HOTEL PLAZA-ATHÉNÉE
23 à 27 AVENUE MONTAIGNE
PARIS

ÉLYSEES 359-85-23 Lignes groupées
BALZAC 225-43-30 Lignes groupées
Adresse Télégraphique PLAZATENE PARIS
TELEX 27 616 PLAZA-PARIS

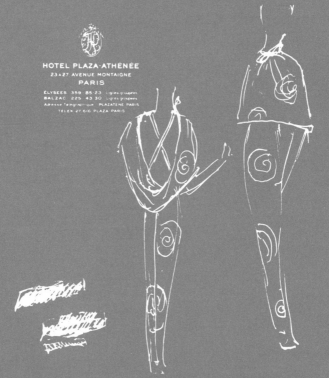

MOMMY DRESSING

A LOVE STORY, AFTER A FASHION

MOMMY DRESSING

A LOVE STORY, AFTER A FASHION

By Lois Gould

ANCHOR BOOKS
DOUBLEDAY
NEW YORK   LONDON   TORONTO   SYDNEY   AUCKLAND

An Anchor Book
PUBLISHED BY DOUBLEDAY
a division of Bantam Doubleday Dell Publishing Group, Inc.
1540 Broadway, New York, New York 10036

Anchor Books, Doubleday, and the portrayal of an anchor are
trademarks of Doubleday, a division of Bantam Doubleday Dell
Publishing Group, Inc.

Library of Congress Cataloging-in-Publication Data
Gould, Lois.
    Mommy dressing : a love story, after a fashion / by Lois Gould. —
1st Anchor Books ed.
        p. cm.
    1. Copeland, Jo, d. 1982—Family. 2. Gould, Lois—Family.
    3. Women fashion designers—United States—Biography.
    4. Mothers and daughters—United States—Biography.   I. Title.
    TT505.C67G68   1998
    746.9'2'092—dc21   97-46573
                                                                        CIP

BOOK DESIGN BY LEAH S. CARLSON

ISBN 0-385-49053-4
Copyright © 1998 by Lois Gould

10   9   8   7   6   5   4   3   2   1

To R.E.G., for the gift of his life and love
And to Roger and Tony — his dear boys, my sons

CONTENTS

TRAPUNTO	1
SAMPLE	7
MODELS	15
MIX & MATCH	29
ENSEMBLE	41
DIAMONDS	47
SMOCKING	55
VANITY	65
SILHOUETTE	71
SEPARATES	87
TISSUE	97
ENSEMBLE II	103
DIAMONDS II	115
COSTUME	127
SEPARATES II	135
ECDYSIAST	149

SILHOUETTE II   *161*

STRIPES   *167*

SEEING RED   *185*

SEPARATES III   *197*

ENSEMBLE III   *207*

SEPARATES IV   *213*

MODELS II   *227*

ENSEMBLE IV   *235*

FITTING   *253*

MOMMY DRESSING

A LOVE STORY, AFTER A FASHION

TRAPUNTO

THERE IS A PHOTOGRAPH OF HER WEARING MY FAVORITE OF ALL HER COSTUMES: A LONG, SHINing robe that rippled with light when she moved. Cloth-of-silver was the material, quilted and stitched with a delicate tracery of birds and flowers—trapunto, she called it. Not the name of a fairy-tale princess shut up in a tower, who let down her hair for her lover to climb, but it might as well have been. The buttons were iridescent moonstone clusters, and though my mother's hair was neither long nor golden like that of a princess, it shone above the cloth-of-silver like a wreath of dark feathers.

Do I remember her dressing for that photograph? Seated on her black velvet pouf, before the giant mirror set between silver columns that reached all the way up to the ceiling? This was what she called her vanity; it seemed to me an ark of some covenant, with hidden doors that swung open to reveal fragrant jars and beautiful bottles, each of which held other secrets.

Everything I knew about my mother, Jo Copeland, happened right there. For what I knew about her was only the dressing. Nothing of the rest of her life was visible to me. Unless the dressing was, in fact, the life.

Rows of shoes, regimental in their order, in their number, lived in the closet. In my room I, too, had rows of high shelves, occupied by dolls I had never played with, each one a souvenir from some foreign country my mother had visited. Each time she went away, she brought back a doll for what she called "my daughter's collection." Each was exquisitely costumed in a mantilla or lederhosen or a dirndl. Each sat primly in its place, to be admired from a safe, touch-me-not distance. Like my mother.

I was twelve when I first wore a Jo Copeland original.

It was one of her own, fragrant with her own perfume, and I adored it on her. I was going to a grown-up party. The dress had green and pink stripes and was made of a heavy ribbed silk that gleamed softly and seemed more like the stuff of a man's necktie than a woman's dress. She called it repp, and helped me struggle to get the jeweled buckle fastened around the baby fat of my midsection.

"Don't perspire in this dress," she warned me. "I never perspire. Why must you?"

This was a typical nonquestion, unanswerable but exquisitely painful. Throughout my teens there were others: "Is that a pimple?" "Why do you let your hair frizz up?" Later, in my rebellious phase, I refused to wear dresses at all, Jo Copeland or otherwise, opting instead for jeans and flapping men's shirts. Then came the ultimate question: "What are you gotten up for?"

I did, of course, perspire in the silk repp dress. She never wore it again, and I never again asked to borrow anything of hers I couldn't live up to.

As for the long, shining silver robe in the photograph, I never touched it. Even as an adult, I could not imagine myself enrobed in such splendor.

The odd thing about that robe, now that I think about it, was that it was meant to be worn "at home." Except for the photograph, and one Christmas morning when I got an ugly doll I could take to bed, I can't recall ever seeing her wear it either. Trapunto.

I KNEW SHE WENT "DOWNTOWN" EVERY DAY. SHE WAS ALWAYS LATE FOR HER OWN PARTIES because she was busy "downtown" at her "place." I was about eight years old when my governess whisked me, by taxi, to the "place" for a "showing." First to a tall office building, then up to a door marked PATTULLO MODES in gold letters. I expected a theater, but it was only a sort of empty living room, with pale carpets and mirrored walls. A crowd of solemn grown-ups perched on rickety gold chairs, the kind that mothers hired for children's birthday parties, for playing musical chairs or watching a magician.

One at a time, a parade of tall ladies, who were called "girls," came out from behind a curtain, and each recited a number: "420," say, or "735." Then the "girl" twirled around slowly, perhaps took off her jacket and twirled again, walked back and forth twice in front of the audience, then vanished behind the curtain. No music, no games, definitely no magician. The audience scribbled notes on little pads they had found on their seats. I had a little pad, too. I wrote down the numbers of the dresses I liked, and gravely handed in my "order" at the end of the showing, after my mother came out from behind the curtain and bowed, after the people clapped and went up to shake hands. Some of them said I must be very proud of my brilliant mother, and I said yes, though I didn't understand what they meant by "proud" or "brilliant." And I didn't much like the "showing."

About two years later, I actually saw her at work. This time I traveled by bus, so I saw downtown, too. It was, of course, Seventh Avenue, the garment center, busy and grimy: sweaty men in shirtsleeves shouting at each other in foreign languages as they pushed racks of clothes through the streets or loaded them on and off trucks. Upstairs in the "place," behind that chilly pale showroom, was where my mother was a fashion designer. I found her down on a cement floor, her mouth full of straight pins, her arms full of shimmering cloth. She was kneeling at the feet of a tall, slender woman who seemed quite bored by the attention. This was a model, one of the "girls" I had seen at the showing, sauntering coolly around that room full of solemn people, who, my mother had explained, were buyers from big department stores all over the country.

Now, here, I felt as if I were watching the story of

Cinderella, only backward. My mother, all dressed up like a movie star, on her knees, on the floor, gazing raptly up at some bored, half-naked creature. The two of them staring at themselves like that in a big mirror. My entrance caused no reaction in either of them. My mother went on pulling the fabric this way and that around the other woman's shoulders, her waist, her knees. She went on drawing the pins from her mouth and fastening handfuls of cloth so that it clung or folded or swirled. She went on unrolling the beautiful fabric from a huge bolt, yard by shining yard. She squinted, made faces, tore the swirls apart, began again. And again.

There were other people in the room now, a woman with a notebook and pins of her own, attached to her wrist by a little red cushion on a strap. And a man in a suit, smiling. I knew him; he was Sam, one of my mother's business partners, the one who brought her a gardenia corsage whenever she was sailing to Europe, the one who went to meet her at the pier whenever her ship returned.

Behind us was a wall of glass, and beyond that a dozen silent women, not young, not elegant, their heads bent over whirring machines. This was the sample room, Sam explained. When my mother had finished pinning and draping, finished sketching and erasing and sketching again, finished selecting jeweled buttons and bits of fur or soutache braid, when at last the shining cloth was cut from the bolt, these women would make a pattern, and then a dress. This was the sample. It would be made to fit the "girl" who would wear it at the next showing. If customers liked it, copies would be made and sold, each with a silk label stitched inside the collar, bearing my mother's name: JO COPELAND OF PATTULLO MODES.

At last the bored model emerged from her silken cocoon and went, in her satin slip, to join the other "girls," all in their satin slips, for lunch in their dressing room.

My mother began then to drape the cloth against her own body. This way; no, that. An image utterly strange to me — even more shocking than the teeming streets outside, or the sight of her kneeling before another woman in what seemed a perverse act of homage. Now she seemed like a figure in a movie: one of those in which a maid steals into her mistress's boudoir, after the lady has gone out for the evening. The maid tries on the gown that the mistress has just flung across the bed. She puts on the jewels, the furs. She begins to pose before the glass, imagining herself in the other's splendid life. As I had never dared to do in my mother's bedroom.

She turned suddenly, and caught me staring. Then she turned back to the glass, and met my gaze there. "What do you think?" she demanded, twisting the cloth at her shoulder, frowning, adjusting the pins. "Hmm?"

I liked it better the other way. I could not have told her what I meant, nor did she ask. Sam, her partner, smiled. The lady with the notebook nodded indulgently. The sample-room women beamed approval from the other side of the glass.

What I meant was that I liked it better before I knew what my mother did downtown.

MODELS

SAM COPELAND, SCHOLAR, ART LOVER (AND IMMIGRANT SHIRTWAIST PEDDLER), STUDIED EACH of his children like a sacred text. Adele, the eldest, had a good head for figures; she would go to business school. His son, Edward, could argue the chrome off a Model T. He would of course go to Harvard Law School and be the next Louis Brandeis, that brilliant dissident who advised Woodrow Wilson and in 1916 became the first Jew to sit on the United States Supreme Court. Eddie was eighteen when this momentous event occurred; his future was suddenly as clear as if Sam had descended from a holy mountain with Eddie's life etched on a stone tablet.

As for Josephine, the last child of his beloved Minna, Sam's reverence for her creative genius was a family legend. Minna had been a pianist; Jo was a born artist. Her mother's soul shone in Jo's own lustrous eyes, like a gift of forgiveness from the God who had taken Minna's life. Sam would spend his own life guarding that gift.

Sam Copeland was a wiry little man who liked to dress up in his three-piece suit with a soft gray fedora and a malacca walking stick.

He was photographed like that in 1922, strolling along the boardwalk in Atlantic City, with his mountainous wife at his side, swinging her little beaded reticule, glaring at the world from under a cloche hat that somehow looked more like a cooking pot. They were an astonishing picture. Those who snickered about such things could guess how the match was made: not in heaven, but in the dusty parlor of some professional matchmaker who wouldn't take no for an answer, like the crafty widow Levi in *Hello, Dolly!* In this case, the "Dolly" had two eager clients: a desperate sudden widower with two toddlers and a newborn baby; and a queen-sized lonely widow with three older boys of her own, plus a comfortable inheritance from her unfortunate first husband, might he rest in peace. If the gentleman in question could only bring himself to take on those fatherless boys, Harry, Arthur and Ruby, each one more adorable and perfectly behaved than the next, then the lady in question would be overjoyed to provide for them *with her own money.* There would be plenty left over to support the additional blessed events that would surely follow, once Sam rose to the formidable challenge of Mary in bed. Lest her proportions leave any doubt, the matchmaker could assure

Sam that he was also getting a wonderful cook, who kept a strict kosher kitchen and a spotless house. Any husband of Mary's could count on a crease in his serge pants. Matzoh balls and gefilte fish. Kreplach . . .

Prenuptial agreements in those days were easily reached without benefit of lawyers; the matchmaker could work out all the details over coffee and schnecken in her parlor.

So both parties knew what they were getting into—and what they weren't. And both parties would stick to the bargain: never to mention either one's former partner; never to disturb Mary's nest egg to provide for or educate Adele, Edward or Jo. This explained Sam's urgent strategy: putting his eldest daughters to work early; using their earnings to train his son for the brilliant destiny that awaited him on the Supreme Court.

There were nine children in the broken, rebuilt and expanded Copeland clan, residing in a Brooklyn tenement. Each child had daily tasks to perform, and no shirking. One night when Jo was ten, her stepmother decreed it was time she learned to do the dishes. The mountain of plates and pots left by a four-course kosher meal for a family of eleven sat waiting in steaming water. Jo went into the kitchen without a word. But there came no comforting noise of washing up. In fact, after ten minutes of silence, a high-pitched wail was heard instead. It spiraled higher, and higher still, until Sam Copeland put down his evening paper and went to investigate. Entering his wife's kitchen, an exceedingly rare event, he found his daughter Jo, in suds up to her elbows, weeping into the sink like Cinderella on the night of the royal ball. Sam lifted the child's dripping hands high into the cloud of steam, held them aloft, and proclaimed, in a voice of God's own righteous wrath: "These hands shall never touch dishwater again!"

Jo's stepmother bit her angry tongue; she might have weighed two hundred pounds, but she knew better than to defy a commandment. So did the resentful younger children and the three older—not so smart, not a bit handsome—boys whom the widowed Mary had brought to this marriage. Those were stepchildren. As in all fairy tales, Sam, like his wife, would always care less for a stepchild than for his own. From that night on, Jo was exempt from menial household chores. At fifteen she would be exempt from public school, too. Sam put her in an accelerated course at the Parsons School of Design. Before she was out of her teens she would be earning her keep, and then some.

If Sam had been a rich man instead of a struggling blouse jobber, might he have sent his favorite to Paris instead, to be trained as a serious artist? That was of course her secret dream. She had begun dreaming it at a time when self-made American fathers—including some who were immigrants—had in fact begun to indulge such fantasies in their spirited daughters.

Indeed, many families entertained the hope that a daughter, if a beauty, might be packed off to the Continent as an investment. Properly guided, suitably introduced, she could bring home not only culture and refinement, but Old World money and a title in the bargain. Hadn't Jennie Jerome, daughter of a rich American, gone over and snagged Lord Randolph Churchill? Hadn't Mary

Leiter, daughter of a Chicago nobody in the retail business, landed a Curzon and become not only a lady but Viscountess of India?

On the other hand, Solomon Guggenheim had lavished one of his family's copper and tin millions on a wild young artistic niece who swanned off into a giddy bohemian life over there and never came home at all. Peggy Guggenheim eventually began carrying on with Picasso, Brancusi and Cocteau, built herself a spectacular art collection, and an even more dazzling array of artist lovers. Would Sam Copeland permit such a career for his Jo? Not even if he could afford it.

Sam was devout, shrewd and practical in equal measure. The kind of man who appreciated fine art if it could be turned to honest commerce. That was what he knew. The garment trade in which he labored so ignominiously was finally emerging, in the shadow of the great world war, into a bona fide, respectable American industry. Real estate fortunes would be amassed by far-sighted men who would move the scattered, infamous sweatshops of the Lower East Side into Seventh Avenue skyscrapers. As the industry grew and prospered, Sam's children would grow and prosper within it. Those two gifted daughters would be trained to earn good money; they would help send his brilliant son to law school. Sam Copeland had never been a successful man, but he would have successful children. By God, he would.

Sam had been on the road with his sample case of medium-price blouses in 1911 when the Triangle Shirtwaist Factory fire broke out in lower Manhattan, taking the lives of 146 garment workers, mostly poor immigrant

Jewish and Italian girls whose fathers had sent them to work as soon as they could hold a needle. Some of them jumped out of windows; the rest perished in the flames. Despite the shock of that tragedy, sweatshop bosses continued to lock the girls in during twelve-hour working days. Nearly a decade passed before uptown New York society women raised their voices, and the city's conscience, to demand decent working conditions for the downtown girls who made their clothes. Finally, the garment workers found the courage, and the public support, for a strike. The rebellion lasted six months; when it was over, workers agreed to work even harder, for less pay. But they won the right to a union shop.

It was toward the end of that decade of upheaval that Sam Copeland decided to train his daughters for jobs in the burgeoning "fashion" industry. Things would surely get better once the workers had their union. But meanwhile, young Adele, who wanted to be called Lee, would start work in a dress manufacturer's office, keeping books. And Jo would start as a sketcher, providing drawings for salesmen like her father to display to shopkeepers; illustrations of the manufacturers' latest styles in ladies' clothing. Jo's drawings were already fine enough to be sold to Sam's employers—or to competitors who might pay even more for them. She could learn to draw a picture of a cheap dress and make it look like a million. A manufacturer could call his line Parisian Modes; Jo's drawings could help him get away with it. Shopkeepers would buy; girls like Jo, dreaming of Paris, would buy.

Jo herself was already aware that in Paris, a poor

orphan girl had begun designing dresses, not just sketching other people's styles, but really inventing her own. Simple clothes for rich ladies—but the orphan girl wore them herself, little black dresses with fake pearls, to the swellest places. She was a sensation, and she had plenty of nerve. Enough to get a marriage proposal from a very rich English duke. Enough to tell him there were plenty of duchesses in the world, but only one Coco Chanel. She had turned the Cinderella story upside down, just like that, and just by being a "fashion designer." On this side of the Atlantic, Jo Copeland had a hunch she could do the same. But she had better hurry up about it, if she was ever to escape from Mary Copeland's baleful eye, and her father's fierce protection, which in Jo's teens had begun to feel more like a viselike grip. It all seemed worse now that her big brother Eddie was finally off at Harvard, just as Sam had decreed, and her big sister Lee had a bookkeeping job, also according to the master plan. Both girls turned over their paychecks to Sam, who used them to pay Eddie's tuition, and doled out pocket money from the rest.

Lee had already met a fellow—handsome, dapper, scholarly Ernest—who didn't seem to have much of a future. Shades of Sam Copeland. But she was mad keen to marry him, to leave home forever. Jo would be abandoned, all alone in the family; no "real" brother and sister to stick up for her against the others when Mary took their side. Mary now doted on her new additions: the youngest girls, Billie and baby Dorothy, but most of all on Abbott, the only son who belonged to both her and Sam.

Blue-eyed, fair-haired Abbott was in fact the image of his father, even more so than Eddie. Except that Abbott was tall and strapping; he would shoot up to well over six feet.

Jo was proud to be helping her big brother, but what about *her* destiny? When would she get to see Paris and not have to go home to Brooklyn? With the first dollar Sam gave her out of her first week's pay envelope, Jo bought herself a bacon sandwich. Bacon! Was it as delicious as Eve's first bite of the forbidden apple? How could it not have been?

Other rebellious thoughts soon followed. There must be some escape from home besides marriage. She knew that her sister Lee was walking into a trap, just as their mother had. She'd get pregnant, just like that. And if it didn't kill her, it would be the end of her life anyway.

Well, it wasn't going to happen to Jo. All around her, suddenly, there were fascinating exceptions. Women who did things, went places, got their names in the paper, their pictures on movie screens. Swimming the English Channel, flying airplanes alone across oceans, dancing the tango. They had men, too, but no babies. How did they do it? Were there really men who would leave you alone?

In the movies there were women like Kay Francis, whose clothes slid over her slim body like sheets of sparkling water. Jo was the Kay Francis type. Couldn't she live like a Kay Francis character, in nightclubs and ocean liners, with big fur sleeves and men who wouldn't dare smudge her lipstick?

On the stage there was Adele Astaire, foxtrotting with

her debonair brother Fred. Irene Castle even had a husband for a dance partner; she never got pregnant either.
There was Greta Garbo. And snippy little Dorothy
Parker. And ugly Elsie de Wolfe, who told everybody else
how to live. Everybody did what she told them, too.

They weren't nuns, those women. And they didn't
seem to need "sugar daddies" to keep them living it up in
exchange for "favors."

Jo wanted men in her life. Just not a husband. And
definitely not a daddy, sugar or otherwise.

There *was* something else. She'd heard it called a
Josephite marriage, after the Joseph who married the
Virgin Mary. It was also called a white marriage, probably
after the Virgin herself. Was it something shameful?
Being a kissless bride? Did it mean you'd married a man
who couldn't be a man? In England, she knew, even
Oscar Wilde had done his duty for God and country, pro-
ducing a male heir to keep the name going. Kings and
dukes had to pass along the title and the castle. Wives
had to lie back, close their eyes and think of England. It
was the law.

But convent-school girls heard about Josephite marriage from the nuns who taught them. Joseph never
touched Mary, even though they traveled as man and
wife, sharing a room (or a manger), having a baby. (Later,
in the 1930s, it would be rumored that Clare Boothe had a
white marriage with Henry Luce. She'd be the jewel in
his crown; he wouldn't touch.) Jo and the convent girls
thought a white marriage would be swell.

Just imagine: a wonderful escort to take you everywhere, give you presents, pay you compliments, simply adore you. Someone to do the tango with, all night. *Only* the tango.

But in the 1920s, in Jo's real life, her sister Lee did get married—to the good-looking, scholarly Ernest. And he did get her pregnant right away. Everybody assumed she would stop working. Instead, she took a better job in Hartford. Ernest quit teaching and went with her. He would, in fact, stay home to care for the baby. He would never go back to work; he would never make Lee pregnant again.

Lee was earning a good salary; she turned out to have an even better head on her shoulders than Sam Copeland had suspected. Years of shielding Jo and Eddie, making peace with Mary, watching Sam cope with life after Minna—all that had made Lee a superb manager. She had a gift for people as well as for numbers. And she turned out to be a whiz at merchandising. By her mid-thirties, Lee was the highest-paid woman in American retailing, heading a buying syndicate for department stores from all over the country.

Men could fail you in more ways than one, Jo always said. But Lee and Ernest were destined to stay married for fifty years, till death did them part.

Friends were starting to fix Jo up with men. Plenty of friends; plenty of men. Jo was meeting other girls in fashion jobs—stenotypists and sketchers, girls who wrote descriptions of the clothes to go with the sketches: "T-strap sandals like those worn by Miss Irene Castle for doing the cakewalk." After work, they too wore T-strap sandals and did the cakewalk. And went on dreaming of Paris. Fashion girls were beginning to earn good money; Jo had steady work, and better pay all the time. Sam agreed to let her keep more of it, so she could start saving. A third-class ticket on a first-class ocean liner was all she needed now.

MIX & MATCH

IN THE EARLY TWENTIES, IF A THING WAS
BIG, NEW AND DELUXE — THEATER, OCEAN LINER,
Paris hotel — it was bound to be called the Majestic. So it
was with the grand New York skyscraper apartment house
built to look down on Central Park's western rim. From
set-back terraces on the upper floors, nestled between
the massive Art Deco twin towers, Majestic dwellers
could watch the first American zeppelins floating through
New Jersey clouds. This Majestic was where my father
would take Jo home to meet his family.

She had no intention of being impressed. Central
Park West was not Park Avenue. Nor was it the Champs
Elysées. She knew a little about addresses now. She'd
had her maiden voyage to Europe; that made her a
woman of the world. Photographers snapped her in a fur

coat at Deauville; in ropes of faux pearls at Longchamps; in snazzy spectator pumps at Biarritz.

Back home, too, she was making her moves. The owner of an excellent dress house had picked her out of her class at Parsons to be trained as a designer. She proved to be a whiz at cutting fabric—a natural, like a rookie hitter who knocks the ball out of the park. For the rest of her own long life, Rose Amado of Pattullo Modes never stopped boasting about Jo, her young protegée who turned out to be a genius.

The rewards were quick and rich. A salary boost, that dream ticket to Paris, and, finally, the right to call herself a designer.

In the American fashion business then, Paris was the equivalent of boot camp. It was where you went to learn your craft. Not only at the couture showings, but on the streets, in the shops, in the cafés and theaters and night-clubs. Montmartre; the Latin Quarter. You learned never to go out without a scrap of paper to sketch on, never to lose your pencil. Knowing how to have your hand kissed, where to daub the new fragrance Chanel No. 5, was part of your homework. The assignment was to acquire chic, and figure out how to translate it into American—for profit. Your boss was depending on it. So was your future. *American* fashion didn't exist as yet—except in the ambitious daydreams of fledgling designers like Jo. For now, they were strictly French Impressionists; that is, they did their impressions of French ideas, colors, shapes, textures and flavors. The *je ne sais quoi* that made rich society women cross the Atlantic to be fitted by Schiaparelli, Poiret and Madame Grès.

For those who merely yearned to look the way society beauties looked in their Paris originals, American manufacturers did the best they could. Imitation was the sincerest form of flattery, and Paris didn't seem to mind. American dress labels said PARISIAN MODES; and Frenchmen smiled. The couture houses could ban professional spies, or even arrest a pirate who filched sketches and rolled them up in a hollow walking stick. But how could it hurt France if the Yanks thought French dressing was good for everything, including salad? If, indeed, the very word "French," all by itself, could spice up America's love life? French kisses! French ticklers! Ooh, la la! Small wonder that in England at the same time, FRENCH never appeared on anything respectable. Even fine imported porcelain bore the less titillating—and rather disdainful—stamp: FOREIGN. But even English ladies were trying a daub of that Chanel No. 5, here and there. It did wonders.

By the time Jo sailed home from that first expedition, she knew how to tie a scarf around her neck and fling it so that it transformed everything else she had on. It was a trick she used all her life. Like Isadora Duncan. I never saw another American woman who could do it. Not even Jo's own models. Not even me.

She had picked up some useful French phrases, too. The notion of *jolie laide* was worth learning. It meant ugliness made beautiful through the magic of charm, talent, fire and chic. It described the unforgettable singer Edith Piaf, who looked like a poster child for a wasting disease. It suited Fanny Brice until she had her nose bobbed. It wouldn't have pleased Barbra Streisand a bit, and now, hardly anyone would put up with it. Even in Paris.

There were other careful jottings in Jo's new Paris address book. Where on the rue du Rivoli to find twelve-button glacé kid gloves in seashell pink. A coiffeur who understood her hair. A milliner who didn't have to. Fabric and trimmings suppliers; costume jewelers. A dressmaker who would come to the hotel.

She began to memorize what she needed to know—and also what and whom she had better forget, fast. Plenty of charming Frenchmen would dance the spectator pumps off an American girl who looked "smart," and might be loaded. *They* might be gigolos. Or fortune hunters. Or just . . . French.

Life in New York, meanwhile, was getting to be almost as much fun as Paris. Thanks to Prohibition, there were swanky speakeasies instead of saloons. Jack & Charlie's '21' Club. Harlem night spots where you could go slumming in your faux pearls. Good-looking college men, fresh out of their raccoon coats, were the new men about town, sporting bootleg hooch in silver hip flasks, dancing all night until the city passed a 2 A.M. curfew. One of the young men was my father, movie-star handsome and a smooth talker. He teased Jo, calling her Josephine (because in the song, it rhymed with "flying machine"). He told off-color stories: What's the difference between a preacher in the pulpit and a lady in the bathtub? Answer: One's soul is full of hope . . . She didn't get it, but everyone else laughed. They said he was a card, that Eddie.

They also said what a swell couple they made. And they both knew it was true. When they hit the dance floor, heads would turn. Which was her idea of heaven. It must mean they were in love. Mustn't it?

Ed Regensburg was no playboy, either. Right after graduating from Cornell, he went to work in the family business he would one day inherit, along with his brothers and male cousins. He told Jo that when his lazy fool of a younger brother wanted to drop out of college, his father had thrashed him, saying he would damn well stay there till he graduated—even if he had a long white beard. (In fact he never did graduate.)

Sam Copeland had to appreciate that sort of discipline. Ed's father Ike, however, might not appreciate Sam. Second- and third-generation German Jews, assimilated and prosperous, were also snobs. They had their family cemetery plots with white marble mausoleums. Their built-in humidors were thermostatically controlled. Even their radios were out of sight, hidden inside custom-built consoles with ivory door handles. On high holy days—and only on high holy days—they attended religious services, in English, at a splendid new Reform synagogue. Reform was practically not even Jewish. Next thing you knew, they'd be intermarrying. *Abie's Irish Rose* was already a hit on Broadway. And songwriter Irving Berlin would soon elope with a society heiress and write "God Bless America."

But of course it wasn't the *German* Jews who changed their names. Like WASP society, well-to-do German Jewish families tended to marry their own kind. Morgenthaus and Lehmans, Wertheims and Strauses and Guggenheims. The richest of them committed philanthropy on a grand and showy scale: museums, hospital wings; later, centers for the arts and university libraries. E. Regensburg & Sons, my great-grandfather's cigar business, was hardly a copper-and-tin fortune. But it seemed solid enough in the 1920s. Cigars, my father used to say, sold one-for-one with cigarettes at the turn of the century. By the twenties, a good cigar in the hand was a sign of an affluent man. All portraits of the men in his family showed them holding cigars; the equivalent, in a royal portrait, of the ceremonial sword.

In the movies, the fat banker and the crooked politician always kept a cigar clenched in the teeth, and gnashed it whenever they were abusing their power. The bum picked up the stub when the bad guy dropped it on the sidewalk. Years later, when my father was president of the Cigar Manufacturers Association, he tried to lobby Hollywood to show a handsome leading man smoking a cigar. For a brief time there was Robert Mitchum, until he turned out to be a bad boy himself, and got arrested for smoking marijuana.

In real life, a cigar was what new fathers handed out with the announcement "It's a boy!" Cigars were what you served with brandy to the gentlemen, after the ladies withdrew from the dining room. A lucky gambler gave one to clinch a shady deal. Sigmund Freud said it was, sometimes, only a cigar.

But young men of my father's generation were beginning to kick the old man's habit, and take up cigarettes instead. A faster, lighter smoke suited the nervous rhythm of the time. That slender white tube was streamlined; the big fat silhouette of the cigar was dark and heavy, like the nineteenth century. You could flash a silver cigarette case, and light up with a newfangled portable lighter.

The leading man could still be debonair while puffing; the love interest could bat her eyes and say, "Blow some my way." That daring line even became an advertising slogan, and it worked until women began blowing their own. What a contrast to the way women felt about cigar smoke, the way a cigar shut women out of a smoking man's world.

Nevertheless, in the early twenties, my grandfather and his brothers thought they had nothing to worry about. *Their* sons were each smoking fifty cigars a day. By God, they'd better be.

The company's brand, Admiration, had as its symbol a hugely round, grinning moon face with a cigar punctuating the grin. It didn't look like a nice man in the moon; in fact it had the grotesque leer of a classic bad guy. You'd see him everywhere on cigar storefronts. He was there throughout my childhood and even after I grew up. He was there in my dreams.

With my father's arm, and her new sealskin coat, around her, my mother stepped into the richly paneled elevator of the Majestic, knowing she was going up to the top floor. Literally. Ready or not, frightened or not. The time had come for her to leave Brooklyn.

She had known it when she returned from Paris. Known it more clearly as the challenging days and bright nights of her life began to change her. She was a successful young woman now, independent; her salary was bigger than any ordinary girl could ever expect to earn. Who earned more, except for a handful of stage stars, and Greta Garbo?

How could such a person take a streetcar home to Brooklyn every night, or expect an escort to call for her there in a cab? Home! Mary Copeland seemed to resent her stepchildren more than ever, now that they were doing well.

Still, there was no easy way to leave. Girls didn't leave; they got married. Jo could hardly flounce off into a boarding house or an apartment of her own, not even with a roommate. Unless you were a bohemian or a show-girl, you lived with your family until it was time to start a family of your own. No exceptions. And it *was* time.

She hung back for months, even after meeting Ed, even after being sure he was "the one," even after he proposed. That innate, unshakable terror of marriage, of sex and pregnancy and death, might have kept her hanging back until it was too late. But destiny forced her hand; shockingly, irrevocably, another bizarre tragedy struck the Copeland family, and it released her. What happened was the death of her stepbrother Reuben, called Ruby, Mary's favorite son. He died after choking on a chicken bone in, of all places, a Horn & Hardart Automat. No wonder my mother never went there. Every time we had chicken for dinner, somebody would cry out: "Watch the bones!" And my mother developed a lifelong habit of picking her chicken clean, carefully gnawing every last tiny bone, though everyone else at her table had finished eating, and all their plates were cleared away.

The death of Ruby was a horror, but it seemed like a sign to Jo. She would somehow find the courage to leap, out of that grief-stricken, oppressive house, away from her father and stepmother, into her future.

Going up in the elevator of the Majestic, she said yes to my father. She would meet his family already resolved to join it. *Come Josephine/In my flying machine.*

ENSEMBLE

MY FATHER WAS OFTEN TOLD HE LOOKED
LIKE CARY GRANT, WHICH HE PRETENDED NOT TO
like hearing. After the flatterer had gone, Dad would
wink and saw at his chin with his fingers massed like a
blade, to encourage the Cary Grant cleft that wasn't
there. He would say, "Let's go handsome up the joint,"
when he came to take me to a movie. My mother made it
clear that she wouldn't have married anyone who
couldn't handsome up the joint.

In her value system, a man, like anything else a
woman was to be seen with, ought to enhance the ensemble. She liked them in pairs, too. Over the years, she
posed for hundreds of photographs thus bracketed, her
arms linked to a brace of dapper gents, many of them
possibly unknown to her except in and for that instant.

Their smiles serve as parentheses for her coy solemnity. Her narrow feet, in spectator pumps or delicate sandals, are instinctively set in a dancer's third position. If she's seated, her legs, a justifiable source of pride, are aligned at a fetching angle. She rarely wore trousers, except at seaside resorts, because good legs were meant to be shown.

Looking at those photographs, you would think this woman was a flirt; this woman enjoyed sex. You would be half right. She did flirt—with mirrors, with cameras, with the admiring glances of passersby. Sexy was wonderful. Sex wasn't. When I was feeling uncharitable, I would say it was because for sex you had to take *off* your clothes.

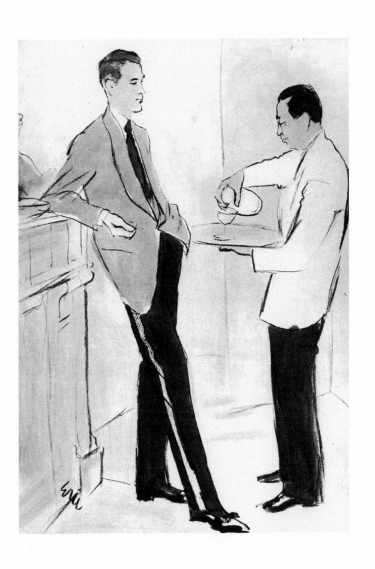

DIAMONDS

MY FATHER LEFT US, WHISTLING, WHEN I WAS THREE. I BURST IN ON HIM AS HE WAS ZIPPING up his shaving kit, and he announced cheerfully that he was going away "for good," a phrase I didn't understand then, or ever. Soon afterward, my mother moved us into a large apartment on Park Avenue, where we were to live until I grew up. The day we moved in, we were all summoned to the square central foyer, a big, empty space whose gleaming floor was set in a pattern of black and white diamonds: my older brother and I; my governess; Sally, the housekeeper; her teenage son, Herb, who was my hero, and Freckles, the cocker spaniel. We stood in a circle and promised never to set foot on the white diamonds while traversing the foyer to reach our rooms, or when crossing in the opposite direction toward the

kitchen. It was understood that we had little or no business in the dining or living rooms, except to practice the
piano.

Those rooms were to be dined in, lived in, by elegant
grown-ups: men in dinner clothes who would come to
escort my mother to the Stork Club or El Morocco,
women whose black dresses rustled like birds' wings and
whose smiles were dark red, like those of movie stars.
Some of them were, in fact, movie stars, though I didn't
know enough to be impressed by Dolores Del Rio or
Greer Garson. I was away at camp when Tyrone Power
came to dinner, but I heard that Sally, irrepressible as
always, had leaned over when serving him pot roast to
whisper how hard she had cried when they shot him in
Captain from Castile.

I did get to see that Joan Crawford had freckles all
over, which gave me hope. And Eleanor Powell gave me
her portable tap-dance board to practice on. But mostly I
was confined to my room, supper on a tray at my school
desk, facing the wall. While far away, across the sea of
black and white diamonds, in the yellow room, or the one
with silver birds on the walls, my mother dined and lived
with passing strangers.

Once my brother chased me through the foyer and
into the living room during a party; he was snapping a
slingshot against my bare leg, while I howled and ran,
shrieking, among the guests. Soon after that, he was sent
off to boarding school, and with him went my only excuse
for breaking the house rules.

Safely in bed, in the dark, I was occasionally displayed to a curious visitor. The door would open a crack,

and my mother and some perfumed lady in floor-length spangles would peer in.

"She's asleep," my mother would assure the lady. "But how do you like the big cabbage roses on the valence? I always thought chintz for a girl's room."

The lady would exclaim appreciatively; the door would close softly.

"You know who that was?" Sally would ask me the next day.

"No, who?"

"Simone Simon!"

"Oh."

Freckles, the cocker spaniel, never had an accident on a white diamond in the foyer. I was very careful, but when I was about six, I began to have an accident every day in school, and the punishment was to be shamed by my governess, in that foyer, the wet pants removed and my face washed with them while I stood on a white diamond before witnesses: Sally; her son, Herb—my idol; and Freckles. Not to mention the painted leering figures who peeped at me from around the trompe l'oeil columns and false doorways. My mother had a famous artist, Marcel Vertès, cover every inch of the foyer like the entrance-way of a Palladian villa.

I doubt if she was ever told of either my crime or my punishment, and it never occurred to me to tell her, or even to plead for permission to wear ordinary white underpants to school, like the other girls had, instead of horrible brown woolen bloomers. The pants-wetting was directly caused by the bloomers, or rather by my dread of exposing them to the mockery of my classmates. I preferred never to go to the bathroom in school, but to endure the inevitable private humiliation in the sacred foyer. I dare say only one aspect of my plight would have touched my mother: she'd have agreed that those bloomers were horrible.

It was in that foyer, twelve years later, that I danced with my father at my mother's second wedding. We stepped on all the diamonds, even the white ones. My mother wore organdy the color of champagne. Her new husband was almost as handsome as my father, and possibly an inch taller. When it was over, my father kissed me and the bride and went off to marry someone else too.

My mother's new husband didn't like the Vertès voyeurs in the foyer; they were soon painted over. But the forbidden diamonds remained until my own wedding, when I danced again, one last time, on the white ones.

frost bros.

san antonio

jo copeland - pattullo "Suspense"

. . . Devastating evening sheath in lustrous black silk satin.   Exclusively, Frost Brothers

SMOCKING

WHEN MY BROTHER GRADUATED FROM THE
NURSERY AND WENT OFF TO PUBLIC SCHOOL, HIS
proper English nanny, by all accounts a treasure, went off
too. By the time I was ready for a nanny of my own, Mary
Poppins was harder to find. The new vogue in nurses was
the German Fräulein. My mother was easily persuaded to
get one of these, not only because her friends had them,
but also because her in-laws espoused all German notions of child rearing, including early and harsh potty-
training (keeping the child on the pot for a full half hour,
until it learns to cooperate). Strict punishment and sham-
ing for accidents were good. Also rigid bedtimes and nap
schedules; scrupulous standards of cleanliness inside and
out; daily doses of laxatives, castor oil and Milk of Magnesia; frequent enemas; and the reading of instructive bed-

time stories such as *"Struwwelpeter"* (Slovenly Peter), about a scruffy child with wild hair and untrimmed dirty fingernails. He is corrected when long-bladed scissors begin snipping off his fingers one by one. The illustrations show the blood spurting, the fingers flying off. Peter learns personal hygiene for his remaining body parts. It's still a children's classic in Germany.

Before Fräulein Wegge arrived, one German nurse after another had tried and failed to get me to eat or smile, and soon resigned in frustration. My mother was frantic with worry, like any working mother of her time — or ours. Without adequate help, she could not have a career. She could not go on being talented, famous, glamorous, independent — all those qualities my father had fallen in love with, and then came to resent. Without adequate help, he knew Jo would be transformed into just his wife, just the mother of his children. He thought that would make her "come around."

True, she had tried gamely — once, on the nanny's day off — to change my brother's diaper. My father had looked on proudly as the little squirt managed to direct a healthy stream of pee onto his mother's fox-trimmed silk negligee. He was smiling angelically as he did it. My father, of course, found the episode screamingly funny, and never tired of telling the story. Jo would listen to it with a pained smile, and an involuntary shudder. Needless to add, she never went near another naked baby.

Years later, when I saw her shrink from my own babies, I began to think I understood. It wasn't just a superficial fear of ruined finery. A child's body, like an animal's, is beyond control, beyond disguise. Clothes were her refuge from the facts of life—and therefore of death. She never touched any of the pets we had. She never touched me.

In fact, the only family stories I ever heard about her with me in earliest childhood involved the head-shakings and pitying glances of strangers when she and my father pushed my pram in Central Park. Despite my dainty, utterly exquisite, handmade Paris frocks, flower-sprigged and finished with intricate ruching and smocking; despite ribboned bonnets tied over my thin wisps of hair, I was clearly a starveling. There is no photograph of me wearing a smile.

Hitler had come to power in Germany when Fräulein Wegge came to power in my life. She had ways—as the torturers always say in old war movies—ways of making me eat, if not smile. She guaranteed that I would soon swallow every last lump in the cold farina still sitting on my breakfast tray in the late afternoon. "Chew!" she would command. *"Chew!"*

She had ways of storing last night's uneaten calves' liver and peas, hiding the plate in the closed compartment on top of the stove until it was time to set it in front of me the following night. And the night after that. The peas would shrivel, the liver turn green and evil-smelling, with the texture of my sturdy brown oxfords. My old supper had to stink up Sally's whole kitchen before she could get Fräulein to throw it out. And though I had spent the entire day in bed for not eating my breakfast, I would be sent back to bed for not eating my supper.

"Chew!" she would say, forcing a morsel between my sealed lips. I would shift the food from one cheek to the other, and back again, trying not to taste it, praying not to gag. The next day, that first and only force-fed mouthful would still be wedged in my cheek. She would fish it out in cold fury. I would have spat it out before that, if only she weren't watching me every minute of my waking life.

But Fräulein was best known for her invention of the clock-and-pepper technique, a simple but effective terrorist tactic using ordinary objects found in any home, and easily adapted for even very young children who couldn't tell time.

The method consisted of shoving that fateful first forkload into the mouth, then setting the clock ticking. The dish of pepper was placed nearby, in full view. When the big hand of the clock reached the next number, Fräulein explained with icy calm, if the food in my mouth had not been chewed and swallowed, the pepper would be applied to my tongue. "Now, *chew!*"

I would stare helplessly at the clock, at the hand as it twitched forward, erasing the minutes. The food would make its foolish move from cheek to cheek; I would try to bite it in half, so that the two smaller bits could hide out under my endangered tongue. But biting released juices, setting off the gag reflex.

As I listened to each deafening tick, as I followed that hand in its spasmodic crawl to the final destination, my tears would begin to slide toward the plate, splashing onto the food in rhythm with the big hand's journey. "There go the waterworks!" Fräulein would say in disgust. This was the only response my tears ever elicited in my family.

At last the ordeal ended; the spoon discharged its horrid load of pepper onto my tongue. I coughed, sputtered, choked and retched, propelling the whole repulsive wad onto the plate, the table, the floor. Fräulein grimly mopped it up and put me, still sobbing and retching, to bed. She was always confident that tomorrow's meal would go down without a fuss.

Once, on her day off, my brother and I were fed supper together on a table in his room. I saw him take his plate to the bathroom and flush his vegetables down the toilet. From then on, I could commit the same outrageous act, if only on Fräulein's days off. When I was about five, I also flushed a coral bead necklace my grandmother had given me, feeling a wild exultant power as I saw it swirl and disappear.

The clock-and-pepper strategy, like the leftover leftovers, eventually proved more trouble for Fräulein than she thought it was worth. Though she rarely admitted defeat, the routine was definitely not cost-effective in terms of her time, attention and dignity. She stuck to it for months, but I won.

Not until I was safely grown did I dare confront my mother about Fräulein's reign of terror. Had she known? She shook her head. Like the good Germans, she had been afraid to know. She had even warned Sally not to snitch. And my brother wouldn't have dreamed of it. *Knowing* would have forced her to act; then what? Her life was already in chaos.

Though my father had promised to help support the family, he wasn't keeping the promise. She would never go to court about it (scandal! disgrace!), despite Uncle Eddie's endless harangues—for once justified—that she ought to do just that.

So she was, suddenly, a single parent. Not a glamorous career woman with a handsome husband, but the sole support of a young family and a very expensive lifestyle. Her work and its rewards were no longer a luxury; they were the stuff of survival. Luckily they were up to the task. Her designs were now talked about all through the industry; other people copied them. She had grown bold enough to ask—and to win—the right to have her name on her designs; the labels on the clothes themselves, the advertisements and the burgeoning fashion press. A woman could go into a department store and ask for a Jo Copeland original. This was almost unheard of.

She was about to go abroad, too; not just for the showings this time, but for the coronation of England's King George, which promised to be the fashionable event of the decade. She would be sailing on the *S.S. Normandie,* the most elegant ship afloat. At the same time, there were frightening rumors about other events in Europe: Nazis, anti-Semitism, possibly war.

If war broke out, it was feared, the French fashion industry would be shut down. Not only in her private life, but in her life as an American designer, she would have to fend for herself. Yet the American public still believed that only Paris could define style.

In New York, Nazi sympathizers were already holding rallies in Madison Square Garden. On Fräulein Wegge's nights off, I heard Sally whisper to the dry cleaner, Mrs. Kaye, she went to bund meetings in Yorkville, just a few blocks away from us on Park Avenue.

Even so, in my life nothing changed. Fräulein's principles of order and control, the enemas and castor oil, the forced bed rest—all went on. I began to have sore throats; my mother in her terror of doctors and hospitals refused to consider a tonsillectomy. Unless it was merely the inconvenience. After all, she hadn't minded my brother having one. Which set off another storm of my misguided jealousy. *He* got vanilla ice cream, and toys, and everybody's rapt attention. I got to see my mother sail away on a boat that looked like a floating fairy-tale castle. And I got my throat painted every night with Argyrol, the vilest substance known to medical science. Fräulein had to summon Sally and Herb to hold down my thrashing limbs while she painted. I think she was never quite so happy.

Afterward, as on every other night, I was not so much tucked in as strapped to my bed, the covers pulled tight, my arms left out in the cold as a precaution against I knew not what. So I had trouble falling asleep. The cure for that was another bedtime story, about a boy who refuses to sleep when he should. His parents abandon him in a dark wood, where horrible child-eating monsters will get him. It's only a dream, though; the parents have gone to bed, and he's fallen fast asleep on the living room carpet. He learns his lesson, all right. I learned mine too: I shut my eyes tight and began to make up my own stories.

VANITY

THERE IS ALWAYS A "ROSEBUD": THE WHIS-
PERED LAST WORD, THE SINGLE CLUE THAT MUST
unlock the mystery of a Citizen Kane or any unknowable,
fabled person—if only we understood it. A real rosebud
is its own mystery; tightly furled, jealously guarding the
treasure that is its secret heart. In the paintings of Geor-
gia O'Keeffe, the bud has always opened—displaying the
potent source of life. And so it seemed to me: the Rosebud of my mother, source of my life, must rest in some
faint trace of her that remained always enclosed in her
forbidden silvery chamber. Must be contained in the
vanity with its sheer walls and sly corners of mirror, its
playful serried ranks of fantastic bottles and jars endlessly
multiplied in the silvered glass. How their burnished,

fragrant contents shimmered and beckoned, inviting me to know them.

I was nearly four when I penetrated that Eleusinian mystery. Her room was suddenly unguarded, silent and dark. My mother had just sailed for Europe, so no one would be in to tidy up the discarded daily evidence of her: those pale films of lingerie, the kicked-off satin mules with their soft feathered collars; the rose-strewn porcelain breakfast dishes; the white telephone cord that linked her to every world but mine.

When she was there I would stand shyly at the threshold, peeping in at the wonderful disarray; the heavy dull-silver draperies drawn against the light. Now I entered boldly, as though I belonged. Something lured me into the deeper hush that fell when she was truly gone, not merely downtown or out for the evening, having scattered her usual trail of a secret life to be continued.

I approached the vanity without fear; without thought I sank into the black velvet pouf and gazed at my small sad face, which was barely level with the low mirrored shelf. My hand reached out, as I had seen hers do, to a large cut-crystal flaçon. The chosen bottle was nearly full; its top was fitted with a black rubber ball encased in silk netting and suspended from a slender golden tube, like some ripe exotic fruit from a stalk. It seemed like a plaything. I knew it involved some sort of trick: press the ball to release an invisible mist, filling the air with a cloud of lovely fragrance. I had no doubt that I could perform this feat. And so my hand swept out, in that confident gesture I had memorized.

What happened next was no more than the usual divine retribution for mortal trespass. The heavy crystal flask slipped through my fingers, crashing to the mirrored shelf, which cracked in two. Fragments of glass flew; vials on either side of the fault line toppled and fell. I sat frozen in an ice storm, a wild torrent of perfume. Dizzying essences of flowers and spice spilled and pooled, seeping and staining forever the pale carpet at my feet.

I clutched the atomizer in my guilty fist as the forces of law and order raced to the scene. The mess was astonishing; more astonishing still was my mute terror. I could not move; they could not pry my bleeding fingers from that smashed vessel, instrument of desecration.

I was bandaged and put to bed, still in shock. It was decreed that, considering my alarming state, no further punishment was required. Weeks later, when my mother returned from abroad, I assume the accident would be duly reported. By then of course no evidence remained. The shelf had been repaired, carpet cleaned, scent bottles replaced. Even the air was no heavier than usual. She never spoke of it to me. The gods had already spoken. The message was not of guilt, or retribution, but merely of sin which, like the sinner herself, had no consequence at all.

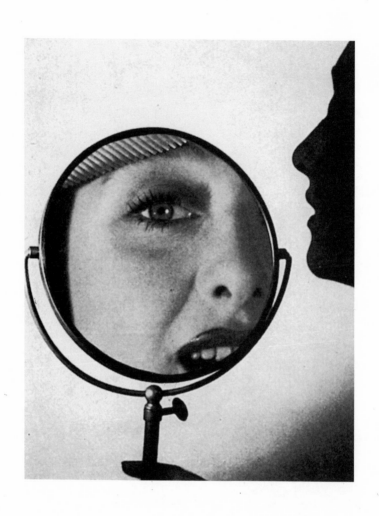

SILHOUETTE

SHORTLY BEFORE MY BIRTH, MY MOTHER
CONSULTED A FOREMOST ASTROLOGER—THAT IS,
one who accurately predicted such things as Lindbergh's
triumph, the Hindenburg tragedy and even the discovery
of an eighth planet. Though my mother always struck me
as a true unbeliever—in anything but phrenology and
Uncle Eddie's stock tips—she took this swami's word
very seriously indeed.

He told her that I would grow up to be a great tennis
champion, on the order of Alice Marble. He assured her I
would also excel at other sports—notably ice skating and
horseback riding. It was probably a coincidence that all
the activities he mentioned involved really nice clothes
and a high-toned social setting. Golf, for instance, was
not included. My mother felt that nobody worth knowing

ever joined a country club, and she hated everything women golfers had to wear. Peaked caps. Clunky shoes that not only had cleats but were actually called brogues. Not to mention the cardigan sweater. Golf could probably cause a girl to grow up looking like Babe Didrickson.

So she was delighted with the news. And on my fifth birthday I received the first of a series of annual tennis outfits, white sharkskin with a knife-pleated skirt that would look dashing even if I missed. I was also registered for a course of lessons at Rip's Tennis Courts on the Upper West Side. My destiny awaited.

Unfortunately I never learned to play. According to my instructors (there were many), I was uncoordinated, lacked the power even for a puffball serve, and if a ball hurtled in my direction, I squeezed my eyes shut, hoping it would whizz past me. A legacy of all the enemy missiles ever hurled or fired at me by my brother: balls, darts, arrows, BB bullets . . . Once he was actually caught heaving a fistful of sharp stones. As always, I stood riveted, mute and shut-eyed. Better the slings and arrows, the stoning, than to face his being punished—after which he would only hate me more. That time he was caught red-handed; his defense was ingenious: "I didn't throw it *at* her, Daddy, I threw it *to* her and she missed."

Ironically, it was my brother who turned out to be a natural at tennis; he graduated from Rip's and went on to the Yale varsity, only to give it up at twenty—for golf.

Undeterred, my mother kept the little white outfits coming. Cunning shorts that buttoned with little crossed racquets. Sundresses dotted with tiny Dunlop balls. Nothing helped.

To be fair to the foremost astrologer, I was worse at ice-skating. Winter after winter my miserable governess huddled rinkside at Rockefeller Center, stamping her frozen feet, her nose red and running, mouth set in a thin blue line. Meanwhile the nice instructor hauled me around the ice for the required hour, dragging my spanking white kid Sonja Henie skates. Eventually the torture ended; I got hot chocolate for not actually crying. I never learned to hold my ankles up straight, or to touch that slippery ice with the edge of my blades. All about me red felt skirts whirled, revealing green linings and nimble thighs. Pom-poms flew and joyful organ tunes filled the crisp, reproachful air. I can still see the rosy smiling faces, whooshing blades sending up showers of glittering ice; the immense golden statue of Prometheus, god of skaters, suppressing its derisive laughter as it watched me clinging to the rail, falling, clinging, falling.

The trouble was that I had been kept immobile too long, confined too much to bed, taught too well to distrust my body, warned too sternly that I would fall and break something, catch something, get something *dirty*. And so I invariably did. I fell jumping rope and in school relay races. I toppled off beginner's roller skates and bikes with training wheels. I broke my arm tripping off the day-camp bus, carrying the copper bracelet I'd made for my mother in arts and crafts.

Luckily these sporting events did not involve serious expenditures for lessons and clothes. The horseback riding did, of course (tweed jacket, jodhpurs, boots, whip, orange necktie with hand-painted horsie). But I did actually learn to ride; in fact I loved it. Horses were wonderful; their bodies, unlike mine, could be trusted to move. Running and jumping: every Sunday for two glorious hours I was set free on the trails in Central Park. On a horse, in open air, hooves digging into dirt. Running; away.

It was too bad that after riding one always came in glistening with sweat. Not to mention smelly. And so when I was eight, my riding abruptly stopped. A city child, a female city child, must not get too attached to any activity that created a nuisance for hardworking grown-ups. Someone must have complained about the stink, or the scrubbing. Governess, housekeeper, laundress?

Many things I loved came to such sudden halts, for similar reasons. The decisions were never announced in advance, never explained or discussed in my presence. I would only have turned on the "waterworks."

Simpler to give away the dog when I went off to summer camp at age seven (no one wanted to walk him). Petey the canary died in his cage. (No one remembered to feed him.) And my closet was systematically "gone through"—i.e., cleaned out—whenever I was safely out of the way. Gone, my Dixie-cup lids with precious portraits of Linda Darnell, Robert Taylor, Lana Turner. Gone, my trading cards. Autograph book with Dame May Whitty's best wishes, and Richard Greene's regards. Richard Greene, the handsomest actor in film history, had dimples and was killed in the war. Gone, too, the news clippings of Frank Sinatra clinging passionately to his microphone. My tap-dance board, once Eleanor Powell's. Even the little orange necktie with the hand-painted horsie.

These things were decreed useless. "Dirt-catchers"

was the magic word. I would surely have outgrown them, or forgotten them, by the time I came home. Of course I never did. I mourn them still. Richard Greene!

As I grew up, the city itself began clearing away more of my favorite things. Pennsylvania Station vanished just like the riding lessons and the Dixie-cup tops. No discussion. Likewise the Automat on 45th Street, where I was taken only after visits to the dentist around the corner on Fifth Avenue. In the Automat, a lady sat surrounded by a high marble altar, like the waxworks gypsy in the penny arcade. You gave the Automat lady a dollar bill, and she would fling a fistful of nickels into the carved marble trough. She never looked down, or counted those nickels in her fist, but there were always exactly twenty. My nurse could feed a nickel to a silver dolphin, who would spit a stream of coffee into her cup. Another would spit cream. Only the Automat had creamed spinach I could suck through my braces, even after a shot of dentist's novocaine. I never ceased to believe that an Automat was the purest magic; even I, with my severe eating disorder (I simply didn't) could not resist a little brown jug of custard that appeared from nowhere, like Sleeping Beauty, in a glass casket, awaiting only the kiss of my nickel to release it. At the Automat I chewed the crusts of chicken salad sandwiches. I even swallowed. But when I wasn't looking, they cleared the Automat away.

And who could have tossed out the grand midtown hotel that had an actual indoor jungle for a dining room? Flamingoes table-hopped like ordinary celebrities. Red and yellow parrots, bluebirds of happiness, shared their secrets in tropical trees whose fronds grew two stories high to a glass-vaulted sky. It was like one of those puzzles in the funny papers: how many amazing creatures can you find in this picture?

My mother took me and my brother there for lunch one Easter Sunday. It was a rare treat for my mother to venture out like that, bravely, alone in public with the two of us. My brother's astonishing good looks almost made up for his attitude, and my perfect clothes almost made up for my alarmingly low cuteness quotient. We would both have voted for the Automat, but that was never an option with my mother.

For the occasion, I was decked out in one of those roll-brim hats, velour, with stiff ribbon streamers—the kind of headgear worn in movies by the mean spoiled brat who always picked on the poor but plucky and talented heroine. Since I identified with the heroine (Gloria Jean as the under-pup, Shirley Temple as an orphan in rags), I refused to smile when forced to wear mean-brat clothes. This could have been a factor in the rarity of outings with my mother.

We had to be gorgeously dressed and very polite, and only once did my brother disgrace her by arguing with the waiter: "Tomato juice, $1.5o!" he cried. "You could get a whole bottle of College Inn for thirty-nine cents!" Luckily the waiter laughed and suggested we try the shrimp cocktail instead. It was three dollars, but my brother had no basis for comparison.

But on my first vacation home from college, freshman year, I took a taxi straight to the spot where that hotel was. I wanted to revisit the flamingoes. "No hotel at that corner," the cab driver insisted. I made him take me there anyway, and got out, horrified. Sure enough, the hotel was gone. There was a men's clothing store in its place. I wandered up and down the avenue, lugging my suitcases to the next block, and the next. They'd cleared away my Eden, assuming I would have outgrown or forgotten it. Wrong, again.

Things and people vanished like that, and not only when you weren't looking. Sometimes they stayed put and changed irrevocably right in front of you—transformed by some witch's evil spell. My mother had a way of casting those spells; usually they involved the living room, after a trip to Europe where she had succumbed to a hideous Chinese screen, or funeral urns that resembled fat ladies with their hands on their hips, but were destined to become a pair of table lamps. Sally, the housekeeper, who hated all old things on principle, scowled her disapproval whenever there was redecorating with what she refused to call antiques.

I scowled too, especially when some monstrosity landed in my room. A landscape painting with a horse that was nothing but a twig—I could draw a better horse!—came to rest over my bed. A massive flea-market dresser bristling with horrid curlicues was painted white and slammed up against my wall, so you couldn't even see my nice plain school desk when you came into the room. I hated these things even more than I hated chintz cabbage roses. They looked like nothing that would be in a normal room, like those of my schoolmates, or even my cousins. Yet nothing I could say or do would stop my pajamas, socks and sweaters from being bundled into piles with satin ribbons and plopped into the big creaky drawers of that dresser. It loomed in the doorway for the rest of my childhood. You could squint in the dark and imagine gargoyles in the curlicues. But there was no chance they would ever come to life and destroy the dresser.

My father's favorite tale of Jo's decorating madness involved the time she tried to buy books for the living room. There were rows of built-in shelves along one wall, behind the piano; the apartment's previous tenant had owned an extensive library. My mother owned no books. None. So she went to an auction at Parke Bernet, arriving fashionably late as always. From the back of the room she caught sight of a set of fine first editions, handsomely bound in white pigskin. Perfect. Editions of what, she had no idea, but she joined at once in the spirited bidding. Fifteen minutes and five hundred dollars later, she had acquired some three dozen volumes, enough to start filling that appalling library space.

Flushed with triumph, she went to examine her prize, only to find that the white pigskin bindings were in fact white tissue paper, holding together the tattered, crumbling remains of dark Moroccan leather covers. She had bought the collected essays of Macaulay, Chesterton, Matthew Arnold . . . No. She had bought tissue paper.

Furious, she confronted the powers-that-were at Parke Bernet, accusing them of deception, refusing to pay. It was no use. They pointed out politely that all lots had been open for inspection for the customary number of hours prior to the sale. The books were irrevocably hers.

Needless to say, Macaulay, Chesterton, Arnold, et al.,

never graced—or disgraced—the pristine white shelves behind the piano. In fact, no books of any kind ever did. Over the years there were foo dogs and china pouter pigeons, chiming French clocks and a beautiful lacquer tea chest with secret compartments. I buried a grape from my supper in there one time, vowing not to peek for three months, as a scientific experiment. Would it really become a raisin? Sure enough.

It never occurred to me that there were no books because my mother did not read books, and didn't care whether anyone thought she did. Yet she doted on the written word, especially with accompanying photographs. She devoured three newspapers a day, and subscribed to a dozen or more glossy magazines. She clipped articles and photographs that gave her ideas about art and fashion, and the art of the fashionable. She read gossip columns that gave her small talk and told her where people she wanted to know went, and who with, and what for. She even cut out complicated recipes and insisted on reading them aloud to Sally, as part of a lifelong attempt to cleanse Sally's cooking of its heavy Old World accent. Sally herself could barely read a tabloid headline, and never followed a recipe in her life. But my mother craved food that café society ate. Brains in black butter. Not pot roast and potato pancakes. Grand Marnier soufflé. Not pineapple upside-down cake. The splendid Coalport and Wedgwood china she collected was not to be heaped with mounds of gloppy brown food, swimming in thick gravy and what Sally persisted in calling "blood juice."

When Sally balked at these improvements, Jo took to screaming—her voice spiraling out of control: the crazy voice of someone in a scary movie. Sally gave as good as she got, at the highest pitch of her inimitable Viennese-Bronx voice. But eventually she would give in, and produce the elegant concoction en cocotte, with the sprig of rosemary just so, the hints and soupçons. She could cook anything, as it turned out. She just didn't want to be bossed by my mother.

It was said of Astaire and Rogers that he gave her class and she gave him sex appeal. With Jo and Sally it was a marriage of style and substance. Their egos were perfectly matched. And Sally always rose, kicking and screaming, to Jo's challenge. When the dish she had refused to try made its debut at a dinner party, the guests invariably pronounced it sublime, and my mother graciously took the bow, without a pinch of guilt. Knowing guests would manage to whisper their compliments later, into Sally's burning ears. But the fact was, though Jo never set foot in Sally's mysterious kitchen, she had clipped the recipe; she did describe perfectly the way it was served at somebody else's splendid table. She did insist that it be made. She *designed* it.

For her part, Sally never missed a chance at revenge, letting the world know exactly how much of Jo's glamorous life was really Sally's doing. And what she had to put up with, to get it done. She would tell all to anyone who would listen—my mother's friends, the elevator man, the florist, the butcher. And me. Endlessly, me.

I remember once asking my mother if she knew what brand of toothpaste she used. (What brand Sally bought for her to use.) Smart-aleck that I was, I felt smug in my knowledge, knowing that she didn't know. She gave me the impatient shrug that meant "What sort of question is that?" She didn't *care* to know the dreary details of how Sally ran our lives. Not only did she never visit the kitchen, she never visited the market, the butcher or the florist in whom Sally confided. She never met Mrs. Kaye, the dry cleaner who knew everything. She never went to Bloomingdale's.

Which was why, growing up, I didn't think Bloomingdale's was a real store. Going shopping in a real store was a very big deal that involved wearing my best underwear (the saleslady would *see*) and being taken downtown, by my mother, to spend an entire Saturday. We went to Lord & Taylor or B. Altman in search of a good coat, to Saks or DePinna for a velvet holiday dress, even to Best & Company's Lilliputian Bazaar for leather leggings, and a chance to meet a Fifth Avenue Santa Claus in whom I never had the slightest confidence. Would he ever bring me a train set like my brother's? Not likely.

Bloomingdale's, however, was only where my nurse had to stop to order "supplies" on our way home from school, or the skating rink, or the tap-dancing lesson, or the French. "Supplies" were big oval cakes of soap, and Bloomingdale's Own Brand toilet paper, and striped maid's uniforms and quilted mattress pads. You never saw a mother in a fur coat, or even a stole, on the escalator. My mother might sometimes telephone Bloomingdale's about supplies, or bills, but as far as I knew no lady went there in person. Only other nurses dragging other children around Housewares or Bedding, and somber elderly women in Red Cross shoes with holes cut out for their bunions. (They went there to buy housedresses, just like the ones they were wearing.)

I knew the Notions Department by heart; that was where you had to go to find a button like the one you lost from your good Lord & Taylor coat. The basement was where the nurse had to go to get thick orange stockings and shiny peach-colored girdles, for herself. My mother wore none of those articles. She bought silk and chiffon lingerie at Saks or Bergdorf Goodman, in a pinch. But mostly she waited until it was time to go back to Paris.

Of course, she couldn't go to Bloomingdale's for another reason: it was on Lexington Avenue, and she never traveled east of Park. Her daily life seemed to be bounded like those cartoon maps showing a New Yorker's distorted notion of the country, if not the world. (There was *Manhattan*—and the rest, of course. There were no other boroughs except in the Rodgers and Hart lyric: "We'll have Manhattan/the Bronx and Staten/Island too.")

My mother's city had strict geographical rules. Park Avenue was where people lived; it ran up the East Coast like a starched French ribbon. Fifth Avenue was where you shopped or had lunch at the Plaza. Central Park was a transverse that you tunneled across to where you had to go "downtown," i.e., work. That she went every day to Seventh Avenue was scarcely acknowledged. She went to Number 498, "the place," in a taxi, without looking out the window. For all practical purposes, the city's northern frontier was 90th Street, unless one was on a train for some reason. To my knowledge she never ventured onto a bus or subway, and had no clue as to how much they cost, where they went, or how they got there. Occasionally she worked late into the evening, and emerged from her "place" to find rain or snow, and no taxis. She would begin to walk then, in the general direction of uptown, until a taxi materialized. Sometimes she walked a very long time, and arrived home late and furious. Soaked to the skin, shoes ruined, and worst of all, hair all *woozhy*. She never wore a raincoat. She bought them, but like golf togs they just weren't attractive. Umbrellas, however, she adored. One in particular I recall was made of black silk taffeta with a long slender handle covered in highly impractical suede, studded with rhinestones top to bottom. It was chic enough to be carried rain or shine. Of course it didn't keep her dry. She left it in a taxi.

Sarong-draped dinner dress
by Jo Copeland
of Pattullo, in black with
tracery of white feathers lighted
by sequins. Exclusive with

Bonwit Teller
of Philadelphia

SEPARATES

WE WERE GOING TO THE COUNTRY. WE HARDLY EVER WENT PLACES, LET ALONE THE COUN- try, just the two of us, my mother and I. This was a very special outing, a visit, I was told by my nurse, who didn't know much more than that. A visit to someone who had asked to meet me, that was all. And the someone lived in a place with a pretty name: Larchmont.

I was dressed as though for a birthday; one of those times that demanded the roll-brimmed velour hat with streamers, the new navy-blue coat with golden buttons, patent-leather shoes fastened on with a button hook. It was a long journey, too long for a taxi. A driver in a sleek car was being sent especially to take us all the way, to wait while we had tea and the nice long visit, and then to bring us home.

Almost as soon as we set out, my mother fell asleep, head lolling back against the soft gray upholstery. Her eyes never opened once, so I could ask her no questions, even if I dared.

It was years before I understood why she nodded out like that so often, at such odd times and places. Once when I was about thirteen, she invited me to accompany her to the opera, stopping briefly on the way at two parties she simply could not skip, even though one of them would scarcely start as the curtain was rising at the opera.

I watched her dress for that evening, marveling as always at the fierce concentration she brought to the task. It was very like the act of designing, I thought; the trials and errors, different combinations and possibilities; different ways to tie the scarf, fling its corners, fasten it with a diamond butterfly. Jewels, gloves, shoes. Bag, contents of bag. Fur stole or evening coat. She might acknowledge my presence by asking "These?" "Do I need this?" or just "Hmm?" Then again, she might only be asking herself.

Many more years passed before I encountered the golden rule professed by that sacred style monster Elsie de Wolfe: "Before you leave the house, always take one thing off." Such a rule, I am convinced, could not have been meant for my mother. The thought that informed each decision, the agonizing reappraisals, the luminous effect of the final whole, the impossibility that the whole would have been right on any other body, any other performer of style, or with any single element omitted—it was all like higher mathematics. On that night of the opera, the process seemed especially complex, endless.

Three spectacular appearances, each before a different audience; all within two hours.

Somehow we got through it, arriving a scant twenty-five minutes late for the opera. An entire row of serious opera-goers glared at us in the dark as we trod upon their furs and feet, their concentration. Shushed and rapped by lorgnettes and rustling programs, we whispered the useless litany of Sorrys and settled in at last. No sooner had she shrugged off her enormous swath of satin stole than she was sound asleep — as if a light had switched off. She never stirred again until the massive curtain descended on Act One. The faint sound of the falling velvet awoke her like a bugler's reveille. Indeed, the end of any act was a summons, a curtain call. There was another appearance to be made, now, instantly. Full inspection. Maneuvers. For this was the precise moment when everyone who came to see, saw. When everyone who must be seen, must be seen. Milling grandly in the grand foyers, dragging their sables and satins down the grand stairs. Exchanging the veiled appraising glances. Every set of gleaming shoulders caught the light. Emerald drops trembled at throats. Faces registered exquisite little shocks of recognition. *This* was the opera.

It took me half a lifetime more to acknowledge that this was also my mother's life's work, and that it too was a work of art. By the time I knew this, it was too late to tell her.

But now, traveling to Larchmont, this sleep of hers seemed not so much a refreshment, not a clearing of the eye's palate before the next rich course. It was, had I only known, her way to keep the distance between us that she needed to keep, the distance that I could never bridge, and that she could not acknowledge. Two of us, alone together in such an intimate space, a cocoon of gray softness speeding us to some mysterious place called Larchmont. She had to separate us.

The house we came to was white; the picket fence too. Even the tall flowers at the door, twice as tall as I was, with blooms flaring like trumpets all the way to the top of each towering stalk. I might have drawn this picture with my crayons, in a coloring book about "the country." Birdsong and the faint hum of tiny invisible creatures; a hush that somehow enveloped all the sounds. A tea table set in a garden. A lady at the door with a cloud of white hair and a lovely smile. This is your Aunt Mary White, said my mother awkwardly. The lady enclosed me in a wordless embrace. I was so rarely embraced; it was shocking.

She was lovely, though, Aunt Mary White, with a soft voice and a sweetness I had never met in my mother's family. How was it she had never been at any gathering of that immense clan? Who *was* she?

Inside her house were family portraits and wonderful, disturbing photographs. I recognized none of the subjects. But then there was one, a woman's face in an old oval frame, that looked uncannily familiar. Grave and dark, very young, but with the same intensity, the same gentle eyes, that I saw in Aunt Mary White. Who was *she?*

Somehow I knew I was not to ask such questions aloud, here or anywhere. After the day ended, after the tea in the garden, croquet on the lawn, perhaps then?

Aunt Mary showed me many more photographs, some in books. They were the work of her daughter Margaret, who was a famous and talented photographer. Was she my cousin? Yes. Would I ever meet her? Did she live here in Larchmont? Aunt Mary smiled. It was too bad, but I would probably never meet her. She was grown up, married, and her work took her all over the world. There was even a photograph of her, in a flying suit. I glanced carefully at my mother, to catch the flicker of disapproval.

But the day ended, and the visit, and the last embrace. My mother sank again into the soft gray cocoon of that sleek car, into the separate silence she required, guarding it with her closed eyes. Did you have a nice time? she asked me when we arrived back home, and she could return me to my governess. Yes, I said. Very nice.

The answers to my questions came by accident many years later. I was full grown before I learned the mystery of Larchmont. I never saw Aunt Mary White again, nor did I ever meet my cousin Margaret Bourke-White. They were a family secret.

The photograph of the lady in the oval frame appeared one day in my mother's apartment. I remembered it at once, and recalled the visit. My mother told me then that she herself had been brought to that house when she was eighteen. She had seen the photograph. "Who is that?" she had exclaimed. "It looks just like me!"

"That is your mother," Aunt Mary had told her quietly. "My sister. She died giving birth to you."

It was the first and only time Jo would hear her own life story: that she was the third child born to Sam Copeland and his solemn, gifted young wife Minna Barrows.

That Minna had been a pianist, a Southern beauty. That after she died in childbirth, he married Mary, the older widow, not a beauty, and took on her three young sons, Jo's stepbrothers. That Mary had accepted Sam on condition that the memory of Minna be erased from all their lives. This was why Minna had never been mentioned to Jo, to Eddie or to Adele. And when the new children came, when there were nine in the family—his, hers and theirs—there was finally no whisper or ghost of Minna left, but one. The face of her youngest child, who was to be Sam's favorite, Minna's deathbed/childbed legacy. Minna's ghost would live on in the face of a small, solemn, gifted young girl who was herself destined to be a mother who wasn't there. My mother, Jo, went home from that fateful visit to her Aunt Mary promising never to betray the secret, not even to confront her father with what she now knew. The burden of silence, of loss, of terror, would be hers to bear for the rest of her life.

TISSUE

DRIFTS OF WHITE LAY IN CRISP RECTANGLES
ACROSS THE PEARL-GRAY SATIN EXPANSE OF HER
bed. It was the signal for "Europe": a word I dimly understood to be magic, the central magic of her life as a
fashion designer. Of course, I knew only that Paris, London, Biarritz, Deauville were faraway places that she
would journey to by sea, on a white boat with glossy black
smokestacks. When she sailed, there would be flowers
and music; throngs of elegant people would gather to
celebrate her going away, with waves and smiles and
high-pitched chatter. Women in silly hats and strange
furs: caracul, broadtail, foxes biting each other's tail behind their wearers' backs.

My mother made these journeys twice a year to "view
the collections" and see what everyone was wearing

everywhere but here in New York. Packing her off was a precise and exacting science, whose foundation rested on the stacks of white tissue and an army of cream-colored leather steamer trunks that materialized suddenly in her bedroom and stood at attention for a week before the packing. Then, at a touch, their jaws sprang open, revealing drawers and closets of amazing intricacy. Hats had a fitted case all to themselves; shoes had another. Cosmetics, perfumes, handbags, jewels, gloves, scarves and stockings—all traveled securely bound by straps and snaps, snug pouches of suede or satin, hidden pockets and secret compartments. But each dress had to be filled with tissue as if someone were already wearing it: whole bodies of tissue shaped and molded to round out the arms, pull up the bosom, stiffen the collar. Sheets of tissue shielded each creation from the next, lest some precious paillette snag a marabou, and neither of them survive.

I watched the process from the doorway of her room. It was like a birth, with frantic women performing mysterious, urgent tasks: Sally, the housekeeper; my governess; a laundress; a woman from downtown who was a specialist in tissue. All of them crushing and smoothing, pressing and folding. Drawers and closets were virtually emptied, their flowing, exuberant contents reduced and forced into hiding inside those rapacious trunks, as though a pack of full-blown, fantastic genies had to be stuffed back inside their magic bottles.

Throughout her life, my mother traveled with her entire wardrobe. The rationale was simple: she never knew what sudden event might demand the one pink chiffon scarf she'd left behind.

In the days of great ocean liners, taking it all with you was hardly a problem. Taxi drivers were courteous; porters said "yes, ma'am" with a smile. She could and did order everything brought to her stateroom; for all I knew, she could and did spend the voyage blissfully changing her clothes. Two weeks in Paris, one on the Riviera, two at sea—and never the same costume twice. Besides, if she decided to run away forever, she was prepared. Indeed, years later she told me that she had thought about doing just that, every time she sailed. I wasn't surprised. For each time I watched those trunks snap shut, I imagined that she was going "for good," as my father had.

When air travel eventually replaced the ocean liners, I suspect she suffered more than most. Gone was the beautiful set of trunks. Suitcases, which she persisted in calling "grips," were never as nice as creamy leather. No hidden compartments. Still, she took everything, and always paid nearly the price of a second ticket for the overweight.

After her death, I received a telephone call from an unknown titled lady in Marbella who had once met my mother in Majorca. She wondered if I would part with one of Jo Copeland's suitcases. My mother had taught her how to pack one's whole life to travel the world, and have it emerge without a wrinkle.

Tissue, I said.

ENSEMBLE II

AMONG MY MOTHER'S LIFE PARTNERS, I SOMEHOW ASSUMED THE FIRST, THE BEST, WAS Sam. Not my father or her brief second husband, Mitch, or any of the long-running gentlemen callers in between, but faithful worried Sam whose soft lisp and owlish glasses marked him clearly *out* of the running, despite the red flower in his lapel, the courtly attention he paid her, the spiffy suit with all its four buttons buttoned, squaring him off like a jaunty Cheerios box. Sam's private life went unmentioned, though I had often enough heard my mother sniff about "fairies" in the fashion world; heard her, indeed, insisting that they were nothing less than a new full-blown species, a race, as mysterious in origin as in physical distinction. They were all slender and lithe as girls, purse-mouthed and impossibly smooth all over. If they were designers, she knew their grand design: to disfigure women, out of sheer malice. How else explain their horrid achievements? The sack, bringing up the rear at exactly the worst point of a female's anatomy. Or the flattening chemise, mannish trousers, unspeakable miniskirt. I flung myself into each of these atrocities in turn, if only to upset her: my first serious success in attracting her full attention.

It was odd that she perceived no evil intent in the motives of gay male hat designers, no matter how silly they made women look. Even her own hats, chosen with great care and reckless expense from those very milliners, bore strange fruit and hanging gardens, not to mention the coy little face veils indelibly smudged front and center with the wearer's lipstick, from the first wearing. One had to eat, drink, smoke and kiss through those fetching little holes.

As to the kissing, or other erotic activity, of "fairies," she would have shuddered at the thought. Indeed, she shuddered at the thought that anyone did it. I caught an occasional, delicious fragment of telephone gossip about some poor sap who had pinched a showgirl's fanny and got himself trapped. It was clear that showgirls permitted pinches in order to spring traps. Yet I knew that my own uncle, her adored youngest brother, Abbott, had actually married a showgirl. Pinched and trapped! Aunt Nora was larger than life—Junoesque, they called it then—a vivid Irish chorine who invariably broke into warbling song and laughter with a few drinks at family gatherings. Respectable matronhood notwithstanding, Nora also refused to tone down her man-trap style, despite her sister-in-law Jo's most withering remarks. Everyone else — sisters, in-laws, friends, me, even the Other Woman in my father's life — caved in at Jo's first critical frown. "Are those shoes supposed to be *brown?*" (The offending footwear never appeared again in Jo's presence.) "Why does your hair get all woozhy like that?" ("Woozhy," an original coinage, signified a state worse than frizzy. Woozhy demanded a turban at least. In extremis, a set of false bangs until the crisis passed.) Never mind. Aunt Nora never caved in. My uncle had taken the girl out of the show, but not the vice versa. Did the pinching ever stop? I fervently hoped not.

Downtown, besides Sam, Jo had two other partners, Morty and Margery. They had all been and would be together forever, I thought — without even knowing that my mother was in fact their prize property, like a movie star under contract to a powerful studio.

I could not tell exactly what each of the partners did, though apparently it took all of them to run the business. There was being nice to out-of-town buyers (Broadway tickets? Dates with models?). There was supervising the sample-room girls, the shipping-room women, the factory men. Dealing with suppliers and salesmen, keeping the books, meeting production schedules, putting on showings, saying yes to my mother's extravagant ideas, or no if the crystal beads cost too much, or the ruffles could ruff with less sumptuous stuff.

Sam, Morty and Margery had identical permanent creases between the eyes, like a trio of governesses wearied by guarding and fussing. My mother was the high-strung talented child entrusted to their nervous care; she had to be alternately indulged, held in check, and shown off. To my child's eye, Sam was the indulger, Morty the holder in check. Margery I saw as a spare holder in check, like Sally the housekeeper on my nurse's day off. Unlike Sally, who might slip me a bit of soggy toast dipped in her coffee, however, Margery did not seem to have an indulgent bone in her tiny body.

I figured my mother was allowed to do the showing-off all by herself. Getting up off her knees at the end of the day, dressing up in her latest creation, hot off the dress dummy, she could set out to conquer the whole dining, dancing, showing-off world. Her hair "done," fingernails red as little radishes, despite the chips that fell where they might—on the sample-room floor.

The elegant designer Pauline Trigère once recalled catching a glimpse of a dazzling creature floating across a nightclub dance floor. "Who is that?" she asked a fellow Parisienne, and was told that it was Jo Copeland, a young fashion designer. "Really?" Trigère exclaimed. "Then that's what I want to be."

Everyone agreed that Jo was always her own best model. Even the partners agreed, though those creases were still in place between their eyes. Why *did* they worry so? Was it really a governess sort of worry—the kind that sent me straight to bed at the slightest sniffle, and forbade me to cross a street alone until my twelfth birthday?

The secret turned out to be not so benign. What worried the partners, among other things, was that they were cheating on the firm's income taxes. Had been for years. The Internal Revenue Service finally caught on and filed charges against them all—including my mother, on the assumption that she must have been in on it. But the tax men were shocked to discover how naive a successful career woman could be about money. The only conspiracy that involved her was one to which many women in the late 1940s still assented: a lady who bothered her charming head about financial matters was not only not charming, she was no lady.

Despite female suffrage, emancipation and World War II, it was still only Heaven that protected the working girl. This childlike faith, and the fear of heavenly wrath for not believing it, kept women from asking rude questions of the men they worked for, or of their husbands—including those who left home without a forwarding address. (The husband of Jo's sister Dorothy was one of those. The disgrace was that Dot kept tracking him down from city to city, forcing him to help support the baby while he played the ponies and sold encyclopedias door-to-door. My mother's family would have preferred it if Dot had stayed put and struggled alone, in ladylike silence. Lots of women did.)

The fact was that money, and especially how one got it, was more unmentionable than sex. Thirty years after the last wave of American feminism, money is still a taboo subject in surprising places. Many a fugitive financier takes off for his tax shelter, leaving a distraught wife who knows nothing about his shady fortune, let alone where he went with the loot.

Jo Copeland had a glamorous career by that postwar year when the bad news broke. It would have been rude to wonder aloud whether she was being paid as handsomely as she was dressed. As rude as to ask whether her handsome husband resented her success—whether in fact that might have been why he left us. Rude to inquire whether he ever bothered to contribute to our support. Or whether her other partners were cheating too. On Uncle Sam. As well as on her.

After long and painful searching, the government cleared Jo of all charges. The partners paid their debts and their stiff fines, and gave Jo their profound apologies. But her faith was profoundly shaken. Could she actually walk out on faithful Sam, solid Morty and worried little Margery? She could and did. It was a brave and foolish move, as if Ibsen's Nora slammed the dollhouse door before she was ready to be a grown-up.

My mother went into business with an old friend, a woman known to me as Auntie Ann, though she was not a relative. She had some fashion-business experience, plus exuberant confidence, a booming bass laugh, and the sharpest tongue I'd ever encountered in a woman. She even cursed. I remember being shocked, years later, when Auntie Ann joked about her own mastectomy (another unmentionable topic), as if it were a fashion statement. "I used to be a double-breasted S.O.B.," she bellowed, to a roomful of people. "Now I'm a single-breasted one!"

I was pretty sure Auntie Ann had a crush on my mother. I knew about crushes; a crush was made up of admiration, envy and longing. Wanting to be with her. Wanting to have and hold, if not *be* her. Auntie Ann seemed to adore Jo. And she was different from Jo's other friends: louder, funnier, bossier, not a bit glamorous. Somehow she talked my mother into leaving her old partners high and dry. They had it coming, after all. Besides, she didn't need them. Was she not Jo Copeland, a success, a star, a woman so chic that even Parisians stared in restaurants, so talented that movie stars and society ladies bowed to her notion of how they should look? I could pretty well piece the arguments together from my mother's end of the phone calls. Not to mention the screaming calls to and from Uncle Eddie, her brother, who disapproved violently of Auntie Ann—or any woman—as a business partner.

With earnings from her first fashion job as a sketcher, my mother had helped put her big brother Eddie through Harvard Law School. Eddie never practiced law, except on my mother. Whenever she managed to put together a little nest egg, he managed to invest it for her in the stock market—and lose it. He was said to be brilliant but "erratic"—meaning weird. I could attest to that myself. I'd personally watched him scoop up an entire trayful of hors d'oeuvres, roll them into a big ball, and devour it like some crazy sandwich. I'd also seen him argue nonstop, at the top of his lungs, through a five-course family dinner, then wipe his mouth with the napkin—not knowing he hadn't eaten a thing. Furthermore, since my brother's name was Tony, Uncle Eddie persisted in calling me Little Tony. It was too much trouble to clutter his remarkable mind with another child's name.

So there were screaming phone fights between Jo and Eddie about that business venture. I wasn't sure why. Either he knew something, or, like my father, he simply knew that women had no business being in business. Whatever it was, her brother's tirades seemed for once to stiffen Jo's backbone. She stood up to Eddie, hung up on Eddie, and threw in her lot with Auntie Ann. They managed to produce one collection and many high-pitched battles, which Eddie called cat fights. When push came to shove, Jo didn't quite trust her new partner's business sense after all. She had acquired none of her own, and came to believe that her brother, my father and all the Sams and Mortys in her life must have known best. At the end of that first and only season, she broke up with Auntie Ann and went back to her old partners, silly hat in hand. They welcomed her like a prodigal.

Uncle Eddie did manage to help her wangle a better deal: a raise, and full partnership. From then on, ads for her designs would say PATTULLO–JO COPELAND, instead of JO COPELAND OF PATTULLO MODES. I myself thought it was better the original way. Besides, there never was any Pattullo connected to the enterprise. One of the original partners had seen the name in a magazine; it was the byline of a short-story writer, and they liked the way it looked.

Jo stayed with Pattullo, with Sam and Morty and Margery, for the rest of her career. Years later, when other fashion stars had begun to license perfume and jeans, hire high-priced press agents to make them more famous, and take power lunches with marketing gurus, my mother was still down on the floor with pins in her mouth. She took lunch out of a cottage cheese container, in the models' dressing room. Like Uncle Eddie, the partners frowned on risky new business ventures. They saw no need for public relations, though agents were now calling the shots with the media. Eleanor Lambert could tell an editor whose collection would be hot, and whose would be old hat. If Miss Lambert was on a designer's payroll, *Vogue* would definitely show up at her showing. If not . . .

The partners knew that if Jo's name grew bigger than the firm's, separate from the firm's, if she could finally sell herself as a solo, they would surely lose her at last. But they didn't put it that way. They said she ought not to spread herself too thin. They said business was never better; the old buyers were faithful; the old customers still knew a Jo Copeland dress was a class act. They urged her not to experiment with new gimmicks like pants suits and other sportier designs. They were, of course, wrong about everything. The old buyers died away, along with the big stores, the faithful customers, even the class acts. By 1970, the fashion business had outgrown the likes of Sam, Morty and Margery. My mother was still dancing with her old partners when the music stopped.

LYING IN MY BED OF CABBAGE ROSES, PRE-
TENDING TO BE ASLEEP WHILE MY NURSE IN THE
other twin bed chuckled at Jack Benny's radio jokes, I
would recount to myself not fairy tales but puzzles of
history. I knew there was something to learn in all of
them. Something of my mother.

Marie Antoinette had on a huge wig, topped with toy
boats made of pearls, when she supposedly said, "Let
them eat cake!" and set off the French Revolution. Many
elegant heads rolled, including hers. My mother could
have told her so. Pearl *boats?*

The Taj Mahal was the most magnificent token of
married love, anywhere, ever. It was a tomb. The husband who built it adored his wife so much that she got
pregnant eleven times in eleven years, and died giving

birth to number twelve. So he was sorry, and had her buried in this glorious marble palace, the Taj Mahal. Some gift, my mother would have sniffed.

Esther was a Jewish beauty queen long before Bess Myerson was crowned Miss America in 1947. When the King of Persia picked Esther out of all the finalists, he had just beheaded his first wife, Queen Vashti. He had to; Vashti disobeyed his order to do a dirty dance in front of his drunken dinner guests. I would have stuck up for Vashti, but then Esther wouldn't have got to be queen, and saved the Jews, and made her husband kill the bad guys. There would have been no Purim, the one holiday when Jews got to sing happy songs about somebody else's downfall. So, was Vashti good or bad? Did she deserve to die? My beautiful, ambitious, Jewish mother would have shrugged: Who cares—as long as Esther got the job?

Actually, the Marie Antoinette chapter would have centered on my father's favorite tale of Jo's extravagance: the night of the diamond-and-ruby bracelets. It was during the Great Depression, before it was even called that. The shock of the Wall Street crash was still echoing in nightly war headlines. And my father came home to find Jo's wrists circled with a tycoon's ransom in gemstones. A simple design, classic Art Deco, the stones set in flat, rectangular platinum links. Almost weightless. You could wear them on one wrist, or one on each, or even fastened together around the neck, as a choker. She demonstrated the elegant trickery of the clasps, and how you could fold them up in the palm of your hand like a tiny set of jacks. My father was horrified. How could she spend whatever she had spent on such nonsense, when his friends were jumping out of windows?

I imagine jewelry horrified him anyway. As far as I knew, he never gave any to her, or to any of his other lady loves. Regardless of those images of love and diamonds he must have absorbed, just as my mother had, and every other young American in the twenties and thirties: the scene in which the lover, the husband, slides the precious trinket out of its velvet case, and fastens it around his beloved's wrist or throat. Usually she is seated, gazing into her looking glass, brushing her shining hair, when he enters the room, in his wonderful dinner clothes, and puts those sparklers on her, and she exclaims how beautiful they are, and he says she is more beautiful, and she turns, her eyes filled with radiant tears. And they kiss.

My mother's bracelet scene went more like this: he came in brandishing the evening papers, and told her the terrible details about men he knew, solid businessmen like himself, ruined, wiped out, whole families in peril. "And look at you!" he shouted. "How dare you go out and buy such things now, of all times?"

Jo glared at him, eyes blazing with defiance. Then she held out her glittering hands and replied, with icy calm: "I've earned them. I want them. I'm keeping them."

My father turned on his heel and went out slamming the door. The bracelets made their debut that evening at a dinner party where, presumably, no one had jumped out of a window. My father did not attend.

The following year Jo bought a stunning flower clip, diamond pavé with three ruby stamens, to go with the bracelets. These three pieces were the most valuable things she was ever to own. Throughout her life, though, she would treat, or "blow" herself, as she liked to say, to other, lesser baubles. "Good" pearls, of course. A ring with a quail-egg-size cabochon emerald. Embarrassing stuff with large semiprecious stones (a topaz "blacka-moor"!), or even perfectly fake ones.

Then in the gaudy fifties, a time of high success, she designed a serious flashy bracelet of fat gold and dia-mond curves, which she wore night and day, and which her old friend Estee Lauder coveted enough to inquire about, right after Jo died. "I'll pay what it's worth, of course," the cosmetics queen assured me. I didn't know what it was worth; I only knew I didn't want to see it on Estee Lauder.

But those sleek, notorious, diamond-and-ruby links rarely appeared any more, from the fifties on. They were somehow too art decorous, too classic and tame, for the rest of her century.

When I was grown up and feeling bold, I asked my mother if she felt proud to be the only woman, of all those she'd ever known, who had actually bought all her own jewels, with her own hard-earned money. *"Proud?"* she echoed, staring as though I'd uttered a blasphemy. "Every other woman's jewels came from a man who loved her. Only I was cursed with talent instead."

It was always a shock to discover what a perverse romantic she could be, after a lifetime of rude awaken-ings. There was no persuading her, for instance, that the Cinderella story of all time—that one about the King of England giving up his throne for the woman he loved—

was a bad soap opera with boring stars, no plot, and a terrible ending. Jo bore a striking resemblance to the Duchess of Windsor in her best photographs; she even briefly cultivated the Wallis Warfield look, parting her sleek hair in the middle, wearing turbans. But the worst of it was that she truly admired the Windsor style. She wanted to be part of that sort of couple—dressing to kill, invited to the swankiest bashes, from Paris to the Riviera and back again. And again. Nothing but grand entrances in grand ballrooms, running up bills one need never pay, being curtsied to by the likes of my mother.

Once, when the duchess visited New York, Jo joined a dozen or more leading American designers who sent the best of their latest collections to her hotel suite, praying she would do them the honor of wearing them someplace swell. I'm sorry to say my mother actually carried around the duchess's crested thank-you note, and showed it off to anyone willing to act impressed.

Alas, the Windsors *had* to be her kind of lovers. The jewels alone. I imagine the ex-king played that classic theatrical scene a hundred times or more, draping his dreadful duchess with the gewgaws they both craved. Unlike Jo, Wallis never had to buy her own.

Until I learned how Jo's mother died giving birth to her, I never understood why, for Jo, a great love story had to be one that didn't end with babies, a home and family. Wasn't that what "happily ever after" meant? Yet to her, not having babies was literally life and death. How could I know it wasn't just her vanity, her consummate self-absorption?

Of course, she would not have cared to be the

consort of that splendid Indian prince who built the Taj Mahal. In Jo's view, that love-match was a tragedy that began with the wedding night.

Jo herself was a virgin bride, according to my father, and she would have preferred to remain one all her married life. He managed to get her pregnant three times in the first three years of the marriage, and she aborted them all. The third, and last, abortion, self-induced with a knitting needle after a doctor refused to do the deed, led to an infection that nearly took her life.

By her own account, not even that would have made her go through with the two subsequent pregnancies that produced my brother and me. What did it was her own father's deathbed wish that she never again flout God's will. He told her that God had spared her life that last time. And if God wanted her to bear children, then by God she'd better obey.

So God's will, and Sam Copeland, conspired to make Jo a mother, after nine years of my father's best efforts. He used to regale us with the story of how she got through labor and delivery. She had a drawing pad and a pencil, he said, and she never stopped sketching. Clutching her belly, screaming with agony, and sketching. She never dropped the pencil until the doctor knocked her out. I can remember my father chortling when he told the story. But when I finally understood her terror, I also knew what made her cling to that pencil. She boasted that the dress she designed in the ordeal of my brother's birthday was the hit of her next collection. True or not, she had created something that night, besides a baby.

And she believed it was the pencil that had saved her. Perhaps it was.

Of course, my father never told us how she got through the second one. When I was being born he was spending the evening playing bridge with his friends Charlie and Red. "Red" was what my father called Charlie's wife; she was by then the love of his life.

My father, no less than Jo, was a product of his time and place. Having babies was not so much about the babies as it was about showing who was boss. He had married a career woman. An exotic creature who had looked great on his arm at dances. But after they married, she was still a career woman. His friends ribbed him about who was wearing the pants. She was successful, and famous. People called him Mr. Jo Copeland. "Independent" was not a nice word when it described a woman. Neither was "educated." My father's first cousin Jeanette had been one of those. Not only went to Vassar and graduated with honors, but went on to earn a doctorate. *Doctor* Jeanette was what the men in her family called her, to her face and behind her back. In my father's voice, the phrase dripped with scorn. And no one had been fool enough to marry her.

Then my father's fun-loving younger brother married a beauty who not only had a mind of her own, but money of her own too. An heiress. She also played excellent golf. According to my father, nothing worse could have happened to that brother. Every day he would escape to his office and break down in tears, like a whipped little boy. Lost his sense of humor. Lost his manhood. And finally lost his life. He died at thirty-nine, of a heart attack. My father was convinced he was hen-pecked to death.

Women wanted the vote now; what would they want next? Young men like my father had to draw the line wherever they could. If you married a career girl, or an heiress, or a difficult female of any stripe, you had a limited set of options: make her obey (the Vashti solution); get yourself a new cutie (the Esther ploy); or just go to the corner for cigarettes and don't come back. Eventually my father tried several of these drastic remedies. But first he did his damnedest the old-fashioned way: get her pregnant. Keep getting her pregnant. She'll come around.

Either he didn't know, or didn't care, that she truly believed it would kill her. She was born knowing there could be no solace in a baby, or any other token of everlasting love. Not even a Taj Mahal.

COSTUME

FOR ALL PRACTICAL PURPOSES, I CONSID-
ERED MYSELF AN ORPHAN. IN SECOND GRADE MY
teacher asked us to raise a hand if our parents no longer
called for us after school. I raised mine with defiant
pride; no parent had ever called for me. I was in fact
called for by a governess every day until sixth grade.

But long before I was old enough for school, I would
lie awake nights conjuring bands of gypsy parents in
fringes and gold hoop earrings, their glossy curls bound
in red kerchiefs, their curved knives flashing in moon-
light. They would scale the apartment building like the
Phantom, or Tarzan on a vine, force the window safety
bars, snatch me from my bed with its hateful chintz roses,
whisk me away—to a real life full of pungent smells and

violent motion, colors that clashed, fierce embraces and terrible noise.

Once in a while my fantasy kidnapping would collide with some sudden shadow in the room, big and real enough to scare the romance out of me. I would yell then, lustily enough to rouse the elevator man, or a passing stranger in the street seven stories below. I was absolutely certain I was home alone. Had I not seen my mother go out, furred and rustling, into the jeweled night? Was my nurse not away visiting her family in Pennsylvania, a family I knew nothing about except that her sister had four raggedy children, one of whom, Kathleen, had infantile paralysis? My nurse loved Kathleen best. I used to ask if she loved me too. As much as Kathleen? Better? She would smile; she had a gap between her front teeth, so the smile was rare. But she never answered those questions. And when her sister died she left me, to take care of those motherless children. Because they need me, she would explain. Especially Kathleen. I envied a child with infantile paralysis.

There wasn't a sound from Sally's far-off kitchen, not a rattling coffee cup, not a peal of radio laughter. No one had even come to tuck me in, the nightly ritual of pulling the covers so tight I could scarcely breathe, yet leaving my arms out for inspection. I was grown up before I understood: I had to be swaddled that way, lest I accidentally touch my own body under the covers, or turn in my sleep and die of suffocation.

But this night I was clearly abandoned. The shadows grew and beckoned. They had come for me at last—my dangerous real parents, and I was afraid enough to scream. With no hope of rescue, or escape, the scream was involuntary. It shook my body as though I were already possessed.

Footsteps did come, of course. Once, in fact, my mother's. High heels striking the diamond hall tiles, and then the door flung open to brilliant light. Shocked to see her, of all people, I stammered and sobbed my preposterous explanation. She did not enter the room, but stood poised in helpless silence for a moment, in that shaft of harsh yellow light. Then she closed the door firmly and made her escape, back to the safe world of her bright living room, her bewildered guests. What could she have told them? My daughter saw gypsies, and thought she belonged to them? Probably not. Perhaps she only shrugged her gleaming shoulders and apologized for the commotion.

I had a few other yelling-in-bed episodes. Some I blamed on bad dreams, and once I admitted raging because I'd made a really important wish, counted to a hundred with my eyes shut, and it hadn't come true. I got punished for the confession—confined to bed for an extra hour the next day. But only that once did my screams actually cause my mother to materialize.

Neither of my parents ever attended a class play, a school assembly, PTA meeting or conference with a teacher. They didn't appear at birthday parties either. The wonder was that there *were* birthday parties—elaborate affairs with games and costumes, creamed chicken and entertainment—and a guest list composed entirely of children I didn't know, who didn't know each other, except for the few brothers and sisters among them.

No classmates or playmates were included, only children who belonged to friends of my mother. Since the ages were disparate, so was the atmosphere. In photographs—there was always a photographer hired to record the happy event; though none ever caught us smiling—one could spot a sullen girl of thirteen or so, done up as a Spanish dancer. She'd be flanked by boys of nine or ten in cowboy suits and police uniforms. In the front row toddlers as young as two or three sat staring out of little Dutch-girl outfits or Chinese mandarin robes. The littlest ones were sometimes posed like dolls, feet stretched straight out, the upturned soles of their white kid baby shoes unmarked by any sign of wear.

After the picture-taking came the games: musical chairs, pin the tail on the donkey. Or a magician, or a Punch-and-Judy show. If the little ones were mystified, the older ones were bored—or the other way around. Then came the food—little ones strapped in high chairs, governesses posed behind them, while the older boys misbehaved, popping balloons, throwing peas. Eventually the mess was cleared away, the guests taken home for baths and preventive doses of Milk of Magnesia. Bedtime was always early after a party, because of "overexcitement." The next time I saw my mother, she would ask if I'd had fun. I always said yes. Did they like your costume? Yes.

But the party I remember best was the one she sent me to when I was eight. My governess carefully twirled each of my five sausage curls around her finger, dressed me in puff sleeves and a bow-tied sash, and delivered me to a room full of teenage strangers playing post office.

The boy who bid twelve kisses for Number 9 was mortified to find himself locked in the bathroom with me, while all his friends gathered outside, hooting with derision. I never knew whose party it was, or why I was there.

Later, when my mother asked the usual questions, I answered yes, also as usual. It really wasn't much harder than at any other time. Did they like your costume?

SEPARATES II

THE CITY SHONE LIKE THE CENTURY'S OWN
MAGIC WORD FOR IT: *STREAMLINED*. EVEN THE
smallest New Yorker, even the crippled man who sold
sheet music outside Bloomingdale's ("Only a dime! Only
a dime!") seemed to inhabit several worlds at once, setting off sparks whenever they collided. I could shuffle
across the dark carpet of my childhood and touch my
mother's silver-fox muff, or the brass plaque with my
great-grandfather's name right on the wall of a big office
building, or the preposterous gold epaulets that Sally's
son Herb wore for his job as a uniformed usher in a
Bronx movie house. Little points of light would shock my
fingers, and change my sense of reality.

I knew that my parents had experienced those same
kinds of jolts. Jo surely had, when she tried gamely to

play bridge with her husband and his gin-rummy crowd, until he exploded over a losing hand, and she rose to her satin feet and threw her cards at him.

And my father surely had too, when he went with her to Paris and sat glowering in the fancy room at the Ritz, while she spent the day feasting on georgette crepe. After her last fitting of hats and lingerie, she swept in, high on the adrenaline that was evening in Paris, and he refused to put on his dancing shoes.

Their inevitable parting seemed not only to split my New York in two, but to splinter it. I knew my father's separate life still revolved around being president of his family's cigar company. Their office belonged in a Dickens novel: a series of fusty rooms furnished with huge old desks for huge old men—my great-uncles, my grandfather, and some day my father. Plus their bent, gray-faced clerks and assistants. Everyone whispered except the lone woman, Shirley the switchboard operator, whose stentorian Brooklyn twang was the only sound of disorderly life on the premises. For decoration, besides the impressive metal safes, there were fierce-faced cigar-store Indians, and dark portraits of the uncles and their solemn, mustachioed father, my great-grandfather, who founded the business and made good when he came over from Germany in the last century. My grandfather and his brothers sported thick mustaches too; even their orotund names matched their physical presence: Isaac, Mortimer, Melville and Bellette. Massive gold watch chains stretched like suspension spans across the vested expanse of their bellies. Their chairs swiveled in respectful silence, regardless of the weight they had to bear. And a pall of cigar smoke hung over everything, like an evil enchantment.

My father walked to work from his new home, a gloomy midtown residential hotel called the Middletown, whose population consisted entirely of men who, like him, had escaped from their wives and children. He had two rooms the color of wet cigar, and a one-piece galley kitchen hidden behind a rickety curtain of wood slats that rolled back to reveal the sink, four burners and a waist-high fridge. A single cupboard held the necessities of his home life: cocktail shaker and glasses; bottles of whiskey; cans of peanuts. The fridge supplied ice, oranges, eggs and coffee. He went out for dinner every night of his bachelor life. If not invited to friends' houses, he liked Child's cafeteria, and the steak houses in the east Forties, especially the Pen and Pencil, where newspaper men tucked into slabs of roast beef that came draped over the plate like thick red blankets, trailing ruffles of gleaming fat.

Friday nights my father and I had a date. He would come up early for Sally's pot roast (she firmly believed that her cooking would eventually bring him back to my mother). I got to eat with him in the dining room, with Sally hanging over us pushing seconds on the apple pie, along with her amazing worldviews. In warm weather she worried about collapsing with "the heat frustration." She saw a terrible movie called *The Helmet*, with Laurence Olivier. About a prince, his father's ghost and something rotten in Denmark. "Oh, *that* Helmet," said my father, with a straight face.

My mother's own date for the evening often arrived

before we finished; Sally hastened to handle him too—chopped liver and a double scotch in the living room, plus detailed hints about my mother's other boyfriends. She laid it on thicker if she suspected Jo had sprung for the theater tickets. My mother would show up eventually, late, breathless and irritable, blowing hurried kisses and rushing into her bedroom to change. Nobody acted surprised.

Then my father and I went off to Loew's 72nd Street, my favorite movie house because of the twinkling dome of midnight-blue sky that hung over the audience. It was every bit as brilliant as the one in the Hayden Planetarium, and more real because it didn't have lines connecting the dots to show constellations. Just sitting there under the fake stars, waiting for the "moon-pitch," as my father called it, was more exciting than most of what I saw on that screen. This was in part because my father's taste ran heavily to Westerns, which made my throat feel parched. Clouds of dust and sweaty men shooting. Women, if any (usually no more than one), wore drab clothes and looked worried. Even in Technicolor the scenery was brown. But there was always a second feature that might be funny, plus a cartoon, a newsreel and, best of all, coming attractions that showed beautiful actresses, with shiny lips and hair and dresses. Even if he never took me to see those moon-pitches, I knew they existed. Someday I would get to see Linda Darnell and Lana Turner in something besides the lid of a Dixie cup.

If we went to the RKO 58th Street theater instead, we had to eat at Child's, which was like the Automat with all the fun removed, or else at a dreary walkup chop-suey joint called Woh Ping. Scalding tea, gloppy food that came in ten different dishes but tasted all the same, and no dessert except fortune cookies that weren't cookies and didn't tell your fortune.

I knew my father always arranged ahead of time to meet Red and Uncle Charlie at the chosen movie, upstairs in the loge where he and Charlie could blow rings from their fat cigars, and he and Red could sit next to each other and kid around. Afterwards we went to Schrafft's for sodas: a Broadway (chocolate with coffee ice cream) or a black and white (chocolate with vanilla). Sometime later came the fruit sambee, as gloppy as Woh Ping's chop suey, only mashed red and orange instead of brown. The sambee was probably a result of the craze for Latin music ("To you/My heart cries out Perfidia"), and the Good Neighbor Policy. My father insisted the sambee was healthy, but I stuck to my Broadway as long as I could. It, too, eventually disappeared, another New York treasure somebody cleared away when I wasn't looking. Soon thereafter the entire chain of Schrafft's ice cream parlors vanished, one by one. Tastes changed; by the mid-fifties people didn't want places with dark interiors, high bentwood bar stools, real wood paneling like the walls of a library, or plump waitresses who served up asparagus tips on toast with cheese sauce as though it were actual food. Tastes changed? Perhaps. I blamed the fall of Schrafft's on the sambee.

Apart from these movie dates, and evenings with friends (or lady friends), my father hung out at his clubs. Not just in the country, but in town too, he liked to belong someplace where the waiter greeted each member by name and knew just what he wanted to drink or eat (the usual), and brought it exactly the way he liked it. The food wasn't Sally's cooking, but it came without Sally's running commentary—or her hidden agenda. At the National Democratic Club, around the corner from my father's office on Park Avenue South, there was a grand staircase, a gym, a Turkish bath, card rooms and lounges with low chairs, plenty of newspapers and silence. Exactly like his office, in fact—but without disapproving glances from his father and uncles. Cartoonists used to poke fun at men's clubs and the habits of men fleeing women. The comic strip "Maggie and Jiggs" said it all: Jiggs in his top hat, getting drunk with his pals at the club or a joint called Dinty Moore's; Maggie waiting at their front door, arms crossed, killer gleam in her eye, rolling pin at the ready.

Summers before my brother and I were sent off to camp, Dad also took us, and my nurse, to Long Island, where he rented a bungalow between the beach club and the golf club. Sometimes I got to join him at the golf club's dining room for lunch, after his morning game. I loved coming in alone, waiting for him at the table. Everyone always smiled at me, and I knew just what to order: the usual. Half a cantaloupe in a silvery stemmed bowl full of cracked ice. I thought it was elegant, like a present. The only other place I ever met it served just that way was in the dining car of a night train to Florida, the Christmas he took me there. My nurse came too, and of course Red and Charlie and their son Billy. I slept all by myself in an upper berth with a curtain, like a stage play. My nurse slept in the lower, so I could stay awake all night peering out the window at the whizzing darkness, little fires dancing here and there along the roadside, suggesting goblins and witches. My father said it was probably bums camping out along the track, waiting for a freight train to hop when it was time to skip town. After Aunt Dot's husband disappeared, I imagined him out there, huddled over one of those fires. And I thought what scary fun a bum's life must be—camping out, and trains whizzing past with people sleeping in upper berths, dining cars where the dishes scampered around on the tables, and iced cantaloupes in silver bowls. The usual.

The third world I inhabited was the one ruled by Sally and my nurse. It had adventures too: Hoexter's Meat Market with sawdust all over the tiled floor, and big beefy men with bloody aprons worrying about Sally returning the lamb chops and taking my mother's business someplace else. And the five-and-ten where my nurse bought her Tangee Natural lipstick and white button earrings that came on a card. One Easter Sunday she put all that on and took me with her to the old Russian Orthodox Church she went to on Lexington and Seventy-sixth. Masses of white lilies, strange music, Russian-looking saints, and a cross with a diagonal slash mark halfway down. I knew I wasn't supposed to kneel in there like everybody else, but I did.

Then there was Mrs. Kaye's, the cleaning store where Sally did most of her gossiping about life with my mother. Mrs. Kaye had a fat son called Stanley, who had pimples but also free tickets to radio broadcasts, courtesy of some other client of his mom's store. When I was about ten, and my mother was away in Europe, Sally fixed me up with Stanley to see "Your Hit Parade." When my mother came home, I couldn't wait to tell about this big event. And also that Sally had taken me to the movies in the Bronx theater where Herb, wearing his uniform that was more splendid than the Northwest Mounted Police, shone his big flashlight to guide us all the way up to the third balcony.

My mother was duly horrified. I could hear her carrying on about it on the phone to all her friends. One of them told her what to do: stop my tap-dancing lessons at once, and enroll me in a good social-dancing class, where I would meet suitable boys.

At the time, my mother's steady suitor, also named Stanley, happened to be a lightweight boxer who had won a Golden Gloves championship in his amateur days, and still wore his golden-gloves charm dangling from his watch chain. Furthermore, Jo had a half-brother in the dry cleaning business on Long Island. This was one of the relatives she rarely saw and never boasted about. But still.

She would have smarted at any suggestion that a boxing champ was not a suitable boyfriend. In café society, her Stanley's sleek, swarthy looks would be thought dashing and dangerous, like Rudolf Valentino. As a sports champion, however lightweight, my mother's Stanley was also somewhat famous. And he must have been nimble-footed on the dance floor at El Morocco. So, no comparison.

In any case, this was a time when Jo was being intense about the airs she put on. She had been that way once before, I knew, when she actually hired a black butler named Buckingham, and instructed him to answer the phone so that Sally's Bronx-Viennese accent wouldn't give the right people the wrong impression. The first time my father called and heard "Jo Copeland's residence; Buckingham speaking!" he burst out laughing and hung up. This was going to be rich comic material for his next night out with the card-playing buddies, not to mention Red and Charlie. Soon the joke was all over town.

My mother wasn't fazed a bit, but there were other problems about Buckingham. Namely, whenever the phone call was for Sally (and with her figure, she was wildly popular), Buckingham would say she was out. Sally lost several boyfriends before she caught on. Buckingham had "the hots" for her. Loud, irrepressible, pneumatic Sally, who wore her hair in a Betty Grable blonde upsweep one week, a riot-red mass of Rita Hayworth curls the next. Sally who broke into "Besame Mucho" or "Bei Mir Bist Du Schön" while cooking, no matter who was in the dining room. And who on her day off squeezed those extraordinary breasts of hers into a Jo Copeland original, boasting "Look, we're the same size!" (Mrs. Kaye had let out all the seams.) Most galling of all, Sally was a middle-European racist snob, who had left a handsome, fun-loving husband just because he was a ne'er-do-well. Not even the most famous black manservant in America, Jack Benny's sidekick Rochester, would have got to first base with Sally. So if Buckingham's flame couldn't be put out—and Buckingham with it—she told my mother she would take her chopped liver and my beloved Herb to some more deserving home. And believe her, there were plenty of offers. Any one of my mother's friends would steal her in a minute, for twice the salary.

Jo decided she could do without a butler after all. Buckingham went, but not before running over our current pet dog, Buttons, with my grandfather's car. We never had another butler.

Certain airs, however, remained nonnegotiable. And they were bound to involve me sometime. From the flurry of desperate conversations with her confidantes, I knew my budding days as Eleanor Powell, or at least a Rockette, were about to end. For sure there would be no further outings with the dry cleaner's son, either. I would miss tap dancing more than fat Stanley. It was Eleanor Powell herself who had inspired my mother to start me tapping in the first place. Among other things, she said, it would help my coordination, so that I could redeem myself from the tennis and skating fiascoes. I was enrolled at age five in Charlie Lowe's tap school, which occupied a seedy Broadway dance studio. Classes of twenty or thirty would-be Shirley Temples mastered the times step and the hop-hop, and once a year Charlie Lowe booked us for a big recital at a garish Knights of Pythias hall on the Upper West Side. We had spectacular costumes made by a professional theatrical costume company: red, white and blue sequins with matching top hats for the American Patrol number. Tartan kilts for the highland fling. We practiced our little hearts out. I had a solo number, because I was the youngest and smallest in the class — if hardly the most promising. *She* was eleven, and had a figure, so she got to wear a slinky satin outfit and danced "The Lady in Red." I spent hours every day on Miss

Powell's tap board, and even ran through the steps with my fingers when I was sitting down. Hop, two taps *down*, brush *out*, stamp *stamp*. My number was "When You Wish Upon a Star"; I wore a white tutu, a big spangly star on a satin headband, and my precious silver tap shoes. Unfortunately I was completely tone deaf, but the crowd clapped anyway. And cheered. I had never been cheered in my life. I took my bow, made my curtsey and my shuffle-off-to-Buffalo tapping exit. My face was burning. Charlie Lowe hugged me. My nurse let me keep my lipstick on, carry my magic wand and wear my tap shoes all the way home. People stared indulgently. I *was* that spangled silver star. I could have granted every extreme request on the crosstown bus.

Now, just like that, it was over. How could she take away my times step? For once, I fought. That is, I sobbed and screamed. My nurse quickly shut me up in my closet, where Eleanor Powell's tap board, my costumes, my silver shoes, lay in a heap like pets who had to be put down. My mother went out for the evening while I was still screaming, but the closet door was already locked, and the door to my room, and the door to hers. I cried myself to sleep on the closet floor, vowing never to learn social dancing. Never. Hop, two taps *down*, brush *out*, stamp *stamp*.

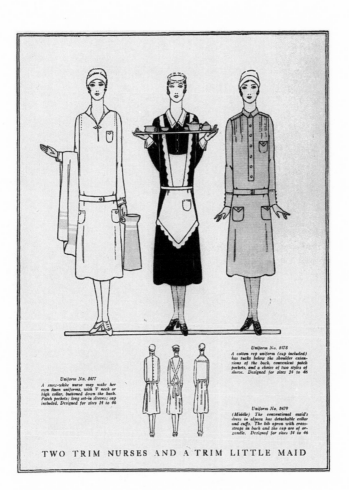

Uniform No. 8478
A cotton rep uniform (cap included) has tucks below the shoulder extensions of the back, convenient patch pockets, and a choice of two styles of sleeve. Designed for sizes 34 to 46

Uniform No. 8477
A snow-white nurse may make her own linen uniforms, with V neck or high collar, buttoned down the back. Patch pockets; long set-in sleeves; cap included. Designed for sizes 34 to 46

Uniform No. 8479
(Middle) The conventional maid's dress in alpaca has detachable collar and cuffs. The bib apron with cross-straps in back and the cap are of organdie. Designed for sizes 34 to 46

TWO TRIM NURSES AND A TRIM LITTLE MAID

ECDYSIAST

MY MOTHER WAS DYING TO MEET THE ONLY ELEGANT WOMAN OF HER TIME WHOSE CHARM, WIT and ambition were all wrapped up in the act of *removing* her clothes. By the end of the 1930s what the Duchess of Windsor had been to marrying up; what Margaret Mitchell had been to the Old South, and Amelia Earhart to the heavens, Gypsy Rose Lee was to the art of striptease. She was in fact the first and only practitioner who *made* it an art. In 1940, H. L. Mencken coined the word "ecdysiast" to define Gypsy in performance, meaning that when she took it all off, she divested herself as a snake, plant or insect sheds its natural outer covering—skin, shell, husk, rind.

What's more, she was both smart and literate: a Ziegfeld girl who could write a bestselling mystery novel

called *The G-String Murders,* about a serial killer stran-
gling burlesque queens with their own tasseled thongs.
Barbara Stanwyck starred in the movie version as Gypsy's
alter ego, Dixie, who catches the murderer just in time to
save her own skin (shell, husk, rind).

Like everyone else in town, my mother couldn't wait
to toast this flamboyant Gypsy. It wasn't hard to arrange;
the lady was already being squired by Jo's old friend, film
director Otto Preminger—whose most recent wife had
just left on a pilgrimage to French Equatorial Africa. Marion Preminger had gone to sit at the feet of the great
missionary Albert Schweitzer, and learn from him the
meaning of life. While Jo treasured and displayed Marion
Preminger's postcards and photographs—showing her in
a pith helmet paddling Dr. Schweitzer in a canoe down
the Congo—back in New York, one could hardly snub
Marion's dazzling replacement: a woman who ought to be
seen in Jo Copeland dresses—on those occasions when
she was seen in anything at all.

Egged on by her life-of-the-party friends, Jo planned
a glittering evening to honor Gypsy in the latest style:
cocktails and dinner for a roomful of glamorous, slightly
scandalous strangers who must all be as keen as she was
to rub shoulders with Broadway's newest darling. Beautiful actresses? She could get Dolores Del Rio, Joan Crawford and the first one-name singing star, Hildegarde.
They all wore Jo Copeland originals. Consummately chic
New Yorkers? She could include the cream of the clien-
tele dressed by her beautiful friend Blanca Gervais.
Blanca's exclusive little shop in the Forties just off Fifth
Avenue inspired *The New Yorker*'s eminent fashion critic

Lois Long to sigh in print for a fairy godmother who would grant her an amazing wardrobe from Gervais's perfect copies of Patou and Vionnet. Blanca herself, and some of her swankiest customers, preferred Jo Copeland originals.

Jo's best Hollywood chum, a silent screen star long retired and married to a prominent California lawyer, but still known as Carmel Myers (she was the girl in *Ben Hur*) often blew into town for Jo's clothes and a shot of East Coast fun. Carmel could be counted on to round up a sprinkling of stardust: Glenda Farrell. Tyrone Power. Simone Simon. Jo's prizefighter was still sleek and raffish enough to include, though he was no longer a best beau. Unlike Gene Tunney, who had quit the boxing ring and gone to the Sorbonne for a Ph.D., Stanley Heller was still twirling that old golden-gloves charm from the end of his watch chain; he hadn't learned any new moves.

Then there was the new man in Jo's life—not dashing, but solid Philippe. So solid that he was to pursue her throughout the next decade, pleading for her to divorce my father and marry him. Jo remained legally separated, an ambiguous state that let her play the field without looking available. But Philippe was an excellent catch. At least Sally kept telling her so, once Sally had conducted her usual thorough investigation. After years of practice, she knew how to dig up what she needed to know about any of Jo's suitors. The best operative in the field was Sally's friend Elsie, a tall, attractive Scandinavian blonde maid and freelance waitress who helped out at everyone's fanciest parties. She was much in demand, thanks to her "Garbo" accent and the way she looked in her formal black silk maid's costume with the frilly organdie apron and cuffs. Elsie managed to flit from one chic lady to another, gathering big tips, secret recipes and spicy gossip. She was not of course the only source. Sally could also rely on the services of Jo's excellent masseuse, and the countess who sold embroidered cocktail napkins and lingerie cases door-to-door, and the redoubtable dry cleaner, Mrs. Kaye. But Elsie was tops. It was she who later broke the story of Mamie Eisenhower's secret tippling. During Ike's stint at Columbia University, Elsie worked for them part-time; it was her duty to clear away the empties discreetly, as she tidied up Mamie's room every morning. And it was her pleasure to report the exact count at the afternoon salon in Sally's kitchen. Sally had been holding court, and serving sublime coffee cake (Elsie never got *that* recipe) since the time my father left us. Even the elevator and door men dropped in, and invariably contributed choice tidbits about other tenants in the building. How else would any of us ever have known that when Roy Cohn dated one of the granddaughters of Moses Annenberg, the publishing tycoon, he kept the elevator stalled at her floor for over an hour after midnight? How else could we be sure that he never dated her again?

Sally perceived this sleuthing activity as part of her job; she was only protecting my mother's interests. If she ascertained that Philippe was a legitimate Greek millionaire, not just another passing foreign phony, then she could plan her strategy accordingly. More pampering while he waited for Jo, to be sure. And the coy planting of an open Kotex box in Jo's bathroom—conveying the message that Jo was quite young enough to have more babies, in case Philippe wanted any. Sally would also do this box trick at parties, in case the women guests were busy guessing the hostess's age.

Whether or not Philippe was impressed, he kept proposing throughout the forties; when Jo finally gave him a weary, definitive No, he went back to Salonika, died of a broken heart and left his considerable fortune to a distant cousin. Though Sally never forgave my mother for turning him down, she kept the box-in-the-bathroom routine going through several more serious suitors, and hundreds of parties. The box was only retired in the fifties, when she saw my mother safely remarried.

But for the Gypsy gala, my mother needed subtler strategists than Sally. Carmel and the soigné Blanca helped put together the swanky guest list. Then she turned to her old friend Foxy—one Janet Fox Sondheim, Jo's favorite traveling companion since the earliest jaunts to Paris. "Aunt Foxy" was what they used to call a live wire, with a husky voice, a ready laugh, the nerve to say exactly what she thought, which was plenty, and boundless capacity for outrageous flirting. In those early photographs at Biarritz, Foxy and Jo huddled coyly in their cloches, pearls and pouter-pigeon fur coats, but it's Foxy who mugs at the camera. The two of them might have inspired Tony Curtis and Jack Lemmon's drag scenes in *Some Like It Hot.*

Foxy had since married and divorced a clothing manufacturer, Herbert Sondheim, and had a son named Stephen. Though she continued to dabble in the fashion business, her later ambitions focused on her social life, and on the prodigious musical talent of young Stephen. She packed him off early to military school, but saw to it that his genius flourished too. What she did about that was buy a big farmhouse in Bucks County, Pennsylvania, near the estate of composer Oscar Hammerstein. She threw wonderful house parties there, made friends with Hammerstein, and nudged Stephen firmly under his wing. It was a brilliant move; Hammerstein became the boy's advisor, mentor, inspiration and lifelong friend. Aunt Foxy meanwhile flitted happily between Bucks County and New York, never missing a fashionable social beat.

It had to be Foxy who told Jo that for the life of this party, she had better pack her children off for the weekend. Not just shut them up in their rooms, which was my mother's usual solution, but *away.* This high-powered crowd would need the whole apartment to themselves. The ladies' furs could be piled on my bed. The gentlemen could use my brother's room to hang out in and smoke. The bathroom we shared (where the vegetables went down the toilet) would be free for the guests; that way the whole world would not have to troop through Jo's boudoir. *That* was the way to orchestrate a party for Gypsy Rose Lee.

Where to ship us, though? Simple. Aunt Foxy invited my brother and me to spend the weekend playing with

Stephen, in Bucks County. We would have to travel alone by train, but surely my big brother, now a prep school boy, could look after me. And there would be plenty of help at the farm. My nurse whisked us off to Penn Station, and scurried back to prepare my room for the ladies' furs. Filling it up with flowers; fixing up my desk as a dressing table; removing all traces of me.

On the three-hour train journey to Doylestown, my brother taught me the rudiments of poker, so far his best subject at Loomis Academy. By the time we arrived, he had decided I was adept enough to participate in serious games with Stephen, who we knew was a serious games-man (he would be one all his life). We would be playing for money; I had three months' allowance saved up; my brother insisted that I have it all on me.

From suppertime Friday evening we played games nonstop until long past my bedtime: Chinese checkers, dominoes, gin rummy, casino, slap jack (my brother's favorite, because he could hit me with impunity). Ste-phen won them all. As my father would say, he *schneidered* us. Saturday morning we visited Oscar Ham-merstein, and Stephen showed off at the piano. At last it was time for poker. The rules were carefully laid down by Stephen; my brother got to agree. Deuces and jacks were wild. The crisis came quickly; Stephen and I each had a full house. My cards were higher, but Stephen claimed victory because I had two wild cards, while his hand was "pure."

For the first and only time in our lives, my brother stuck up for me. There was a lot of money in the pot. The

dispute escalated into a fight—threats, fists and screaming. My brother yelled at me to get my suitcase; we
weren't staying in that house one more minute.

Without another word to Stephen, my brother summoned a taxi. We caught the last train back to New York.

It was Saturday night; by the time we arrived, my
mother's party would be in full swing. If we gave this a
thought, we didn't care. We marched in there like war
veterans, as if we expected a hero's welcome. The place
was crammed with people—women in gorgeous cocktail
dresses and evening gowns, men in dinner jackets and
black tie. Highball glasses and cigarettes were waving;
everyone was talking and laughing at once. Sally, Elsie
and two extra maids, dressed in those fancy French-maid
outfits, sashayed in and out of the kitchen like figurines
on a chiming clock, brandishing silver trays. The black
and white foyer was ablaze with flower arrangements, and
music seeped out of the walls, as in a rich movie.

Making our way past that furiously swinging kitchen
door, we could see the pantry piled high with every pot
and pan, every dazzlingly polished piece of silver we
owned. Still we marched on, through the noise and the
smoke, until we saw our mother, and she saw us. The
crowd parted like waves of the Red Sea. There was a
deafening silence. We stood there, filthy from our long
train ride, full of the righteous wrath we had carried all
the way from Pennsylvania. We couldn't wait to spill our
news. Heads turned toward Jo, frozen in horror at the
sight of us. Drinks and cigarettes stopped in midair as my
brother explained, in ringing tones, what we were doing
there: "Stevie Sondheim *cheats!*"

There was barely a beat of hesitation as the full import sank in. Then the entire room erupted in laughter. I cannot swear that Aunt Foxy laughed, but the rest of that brilliant crowd was convulsed for several minutes. Still my mother stood mute with shock. Less upset, I knew, by our remarkable adventure, the suddenness of our appearance, the explosive power of my brother's words, than by the simple, amazing fact of our crashing her magnificent party dressed as we were in rumpled sweaters, falling-down socks, and hair that hadn't been combed since Friday.

Luckily for us, the guest of honor had all but dissolved in peals of delighted, musical laughter. These two ragamuffins and their preposterous entrance! Their mother's horrified reaction! We were the high point of Gypsy's evening. Possibly we had struck some chord of memory, reminding her of a scene in her own stormy childhood, when she was gawky Louise Hovick, pitting her will against that of her indomitable, fiercely ambitious mother, Mama Rose. It was a childhood she would later recall in agonizing detail in her autobiography, *Gypsy*. That story would become a great Broadway musical, and then a movie, with a powerful happy ending: the child becomes a success on her own terms, strong enough to forgive, to embrace the mother. *Gypsy*'s wonderful, terrifying lyrics would be written by Stephen Sondheim.

I FIRST NOTICED HER LOVELY BREASTS WHEN I WAS NEARLY ELEVEN. I'D SEEN THEM BEFORE, every time she sat on the velvet pouf to put on her face. She would emerge from the bathtub and wrap a white towel around herself, tucking a corner in on one side. The way she wrapped it left the top of her completely bare. As if Dorothy Lamour's sarong started below her celebrated bosom. That towel of my mother's never came undone where she anchored it. I spent years practicing the technique before I figured it out.

But one day I found myself studying my mother's naked body, appraising it, comparing it to mine. "What's that *crease?*" I suddenly asked, pointing. It was a deep indentation in her back, on the right side. As if she'd been folded there. She hiked up the towel, to no avail. The crease was nearly a foot long.

"I had a rib taken out," she said. Matter-of-fact. She, with her horror of doctors, of hospitals!

"Why?"

"To make my waist narrower. Young women had to do that. To make the clothes of the time lie closer to the body." She gestured as though she were drawing lines down a bolt of cloth.

I was dumbstruck. Women cut themselves up on purpose? She did? Redesigned her body, like a dress?

She finished putting on her makeup, using a brush to outline her perfect upper lip. Then the swansdown puff that sent clouds of smelly pink powder into the air. I wrinkled my nose, and went back to studying the breasts.

"How come you don't wear a bra?"

She frowned, but gave me a straight answer. Bras had straps and hooks, elastics, fasteners. These things made bulges in clothes. The dresses she designed and wore had proper underpinnings that assured proper fit. All one needed was a girdle to hold up stockings and flatten the stomach.

"What if you had big floppy breasts like Sally?"

Sally in the bathtub, her breasts released from their punishing D-cup cages, resembled a family of seals sunning themselves on a rock. Great buoyant things, with lives of their own. Dirigibles, sailing.

My mother had no answer to that. She was pleased with her small round breasts, I could tell. The pleasure had to do with how they looked in clothes.

The next day in school, my best friend and I hid in a

cubicle in the bathroom to talk about breasts, and bras. She pulled up her shirt. She was "developing." Her father called them sugar lumps. Her mother was going with her, after school, to shop for a bra.

I wasn't developing. I wasn't at all sure I wanted to. Sugar lumps!

Pattullo - Jo Copeland

Harzfeld's

Petticoat Lane, Kansas City

STRIPES

NOT UNTIL HERB WAS DRAFTED DID I UNDER-
STAND THE PHRASE: "DON'T YOU KNOW THERE'S A
war on?" The Army had already taken two of my uncles—
the one who had spent years running out on his wife and
creditors; the other who had managed both not to graduate from college, and not to find gainful employment,
even in the family business.

One night my father mistakenly took me to a movie in
which a peasant woman sat knitting a sweater for her
strapping soldier son. A bad guy in uniform knocks at the
door to deliver a small box; inside are her son's ashes.
Her gaze travels from the little box to the big sweater in
her hands; then she screams. My father had to carry me,
screaming too, from the theater. Still I didn't connect the
horror of that scene to "There's a *war* on!"

Only the disappearance of Herb was a direct blow to the heart. I vowed to grow up fast while he was gone, so he could come back, marry me and take me away, like the gypsy kidnappers I used to pray for. He promised only to send V-mail letters with XXX's on them, and four-inch V-recordings of his voice singing all the words to "Mairzy Doats."

It seemed clear that I cared more than Sally did, because she was only his mother, and besides, she was my mother's cook. She would have to care about other things: sugar, coffee and meat shortages; ration books and the inevitable decline of formal dinner parties. The end of Viennese pastry, French sauces, even apple pie à la mode. The cocktail party loomed: fancy mixed drinks, heavy drinkers; too many people standing around knocking expensive glasses off tables, crowding each other so you could barely see the intricate jet beading on those new short evening dresses. And not enough help. In fact, everyone said, there would soon be no help at all. Maids would all quit to work in defense plants instead—for shorter hours, better pay, evenings free, patriotic duty and the sudden bright promise of not putting on those little black French maids' outfits, ever again.

If Sally herself ever entertained such an option, she never let on. But when my last governess left to marry her late sister's whole family, I knew she would not be replaced. That would be my rite of passage: at last, a room of my own. Privacy. Permission to cross the street. When I left for school in the morning, my breakfast would be laid out on the kitchen table. No one to watch me eat it. If it was my birthday, there would also be a box, containing a party dress and an envelope with a war bond. I could thank my mother when she came dashing in after work to change for the evening. I could thank my father on the telephone.

When I came home from school, no one would be there but Sally. And Sally, with her new platinum pompadour, would hardly be there for me. It was decreed that I would not bring schoolmates home to play in an unsupervised apartment. Privacy was to be isolation.

The war would change my mother's life too, as subtly, as sinuously, as a fall of black satin over a column of black wool crepe. Isolated and trivial as a world of fashion might seem to a real world in flames, there had to be vibrant life on the home front. For the troops' morale, if nothing else, American women could not all turn into Rosie the Riveter in overalls and snood, swinging her tin lunchpail to the tune of "I'll Walk Alone."

True, lights would be dimmed on Times Square skyscrapers, for fear of attracting German U-boats. But the Roseland Ballroom must stay open for business, and every serviceman on leave needed to dance with a doll who could still doll up—like Betty Grable.

In the echoing halls of Hunter Elementary School, we would huddle during blackouts and air-raid drills, waiting for the all-clear siren, clapping bravely to endless choruses of "Deep in the Heart of Texas."

Outside, the restless city would be changing again. One day the double-decker bus vanished from Fifth Avenue. Riding on that open upper deck used to be a movie cliché for showing nice young couples falling in love; it was exactly where they did it. And like the Staten Island

Ferry, it was pure New York romance for only a nickel. For me, the double-decker was the best fun you could have while moving through the city—until my governess was struck in the eye by a bullet from a BB gun fired out of a Fifth Avenue window. She didn't lose the eye, but I lost my seat on the open deck. From then on we had to ride safely shut in, on the lower. I didn't see why, either; BB guns were being fired out of windows everywhere. My brother used to shoot his out of *my* window, into the lady's bathroom across the street. He figured firing from my room was a perfect alibi, in case the lady ever pointed the cops to where the shot came from. Nobody ever came over to grill me.

The Third Avenue El (for "elevated train") also disappeared; where would the drunken bums go to loiter now? With my new freedom, I myself could venture into the uncharted, dangerous territory east of Third Avenue to visit a classmate after school. Rita lived in a tenement walkup, with a grandmother who yelled nonstop in a foreign language, and hung laundry on a string across the kitchen ceiling. But together Rita and I did daring things there, in her room, like sending away for a book called *The Art of Kissing,* which arrived as promised in a plain brown wrapper, and revealed a dozen different shapes of lips, plus instructions on how they could be brushed, nibbled, smacked. We would practice them all with enormous excitement. At home, I would never mention where Rita lived, or what we did together after school, besides homework. Not that my mother would ever have asked.

For her, there were to be more momentous sources of anxiety. Paris was suddenly off the map, and with it everything a designer leaned on for inspiration, guidance, reassurance. The world's most beautiful ocean liner, on which she had sailed, would lie in a smoldering ruin on the New York waterfront, a potent symbol of disconnection. Stripped down and painted like a troop ship before being sent to the U.S. for safety, the *S.S. Normandie* would in fact never sail again for France, carrying American design pilgrims to the shrine of haute couture. Jo and her fellow pioneers would be stranded at home for "the duration," as everyone called it. Sink or swim, they were on their own. Oh, they could travel to California, Bermuda, Mexico, for ideas. Then they would learn to carry them out with less of everything they thought they needed: wool and silk; nylon and leather; metal zippers, hooks and eyes—even elastic girdles. These things would all be needed for the war.

The actress Veronica Lake would have to cut her long blonde hair so that American women wouldn't catch their own peekaboo bangs in defense plant machinery, thus slowing down the war effort. Menacing signs and slogans would appear on the walls of restaurants, even the Automat: LOOSE LIPS SINK SHIPS!

And the government would pass a strict new law known as L-85, telling makers of fashion what they simply could not do; challenging them to do the impossible instead. Designers would take the dare, brilliantly, proving for the first time that in America less could in fact be more. No pleats, pockets, cuffs, full skirts? Claire McCardell would invent the wraparound, a dress tied together with a thong, and it would be simply elegant. Leather shortage? Women would kick off their heels and put on ballet slippers, drawing "seams" with eyebrow pencil down the backs of their naked legs. No trimmings? Silk and wool limits? Jo Copeland would create the classic tailored daytime ensemble that could turn into a sparkling dinner dress with the flick of a collarless jacket. There would be "separates," created equal. New Yorkers would begin to blur the fine lines between dressing up and dressing down; between town and country, sport and flirty; between patriotic and glamorous, thrifty and smart, 9 A.M. and midnight.

It was to be the end of many rules that had once seemed immutable. Even my Friday night dates with my father came to an abrupt halt. I now had the hateful social-dancing class that night, and he had too many troubles to make it any other time. His father, my grandfather, had died suddenly, leaving a mountain of debt and family dishonor, instead of a thriving business and a private fortune. My father now had no inheritance, only a job. Humiliation. And worst of all, he had to move his mother out of what she thought was her lifelong home at the Majestic; he had to fire her servants and sell everything she owned — the ermine opera cape, the pearl choker, the heirloom German silver, the platinum lorgnette, the polar bear rug I used to ride in her living room, whispering secrets into its ear. She begged to be allowed to keep a trinket to bequeath to each of her granddaughters: my cousin Ann and me. But my father stood firm; everything must go to help repay her in-laws, his widowed aunts and cousins, every last dime his father had stolen from the company safe and lost betting on "the ponies."

My father had a faithful Japanese valet, Tom, who brushed his fine suits and fixed his drink exactly right, scrambled the eggs, squeezed the oranges, and smiled at me when I was brought to visit. Tom was the butt of many jokes between my father and Red and Uncle Charlie. My father found it especially amusing when Tom's father sent Tom a wife all the way from Tokyo. How could Tom consent to marry her? A mail-order bride? Tom would stare at my father, uncomprehending. "My father knows what is needed," he would explain. "My father will choose the best wife for me. As his father chose his wife for him." Tom would end with his soft, self-deprecating chuckle. "Japs!" said my father, each time he told the story. Everyone understood that the story, this couple, were meant to be a sarcastic comment about my father's own wife, my mother, about the foolishness of love, or of marrying for it.

One day when I visited my father, he greeted me at the door himself. "Where's Tom?" I asked. My father seemed uncomfortable; the place was in disarray. "Gone," he said, brusquely. "Tom is gone."

How come? Gone where? Gone for good?

"Japs," he muttered, turning his back to me. He went to fix his own drink at his little bar, to open his own jar of peanuts.

I was meant to assume that faithful Tom had walked out on him, just like that. Whistling? Packing his suitcase? Tom, who had served my father since before I was born?

Years later I learned that Tom had in fact been taken away, sent to an internment camp. We were at war with

"Japs." My father had turned Tom in, voluntarily, had made no protest when they came for him, made no inquiry about him. Never knew what became of him, or his wife, that perfect wife his father had sent to him. People just went away; I understood. Packing their suitcases. Whistling.

In bitter despair, my father consulted a psychiatrist, who advised him to rethink his life. Including the long-running, unresolved love affair with Red. Give her an ultimatum, the doctor said. She leaves her husband to marry you, or you leave her and find yourself a real partner. And when you tell her that, mean it.

My father tried to follow the doctor's sensible advice—and lost Red too. Now he was truly alone, as alone as I was. His friend Lou urged him to do what Lou had done to change his life: enroll in an Arthur Murray Dance Studio and find himself a cute dance partner. Lou would show my father all the fancy steps he had learned—a-one and a-two—humming the songs, holding one arm against his belly as if he were squeezing a real live redhead. My father called Lou "the ham what am," and laughed him off—especially when Lou actually married one of those dance-hall girls and sashayed off to Florida. For the life of him, my father couldn't follow Lou's footsteps: a-one and a-two.

As for me, I was rethinking life too. For one thing, I was failing social dancing. That is, I couldn't get the hang of dancing with, flirting with, talking with, listening to, or attracting, boys. I could win spelling bees in school, get straight A's and skip whole grades in a single bound, but I soon learned that these very things were what made me such a flop. I had begun to console myself with Mounds bars; I had begun to read the dictionary and translate sorrowful Latin love poems; I had begun to write stupid fan letters to ice-hockey players, and to cry in my closet, wishing I were old enough to wear a pompadour, so I could join the swooning, rioting bobby-soxers stampeding the Paramount Theater for a glimpse of Frank Sinatra.

My best friend, Sue, the one whose father had nick-named her budding breasts "sugar lumps," had also developed a terrific giggle that traveled the whole musical scale, Do to Do. She was also a knockout; the boys in dancing school, and later at proms, would stuff their pockets with ice cubes from the water cooler to drop down Sue's sweetheart neckline, just to watch her squirm, and hear that irresistible laugh. I watched with fascination from behind my high shirtwaist collar (the only thing that would hide my freckles). By the time I went to a prom, I forced my mother to find me the only dress in the universe with long sleeves and a Chinese collar that buttoned all the way up to the throat. It was a beautiful dress, ice-blue watered silk, with a train. I looked terrific hugging the wall while the ice-cube queen (and every other girl) went strapless. Her giggle floated over the dance floor like soap bubbles with captive rainbows; like pure delight. Ah, they told me, what a flop you are.

My mother knew something was wrong long before that. I was all of eleven when the director of the dancing school told her, and when her friends who had daughters began boasting about how popular those daughters were.

Then my Aunt Mildred chimed in. Mildred had managed to get a young camp counselor fired from her job for "molesting" her daughter, my cousin, on the canoeing dock. (My cousin had, in fact, been the envy of everyone in camp—including me—that summer; she was the only one of us who had ever managed to wangle a real kiss on the mouth from her crush.)

This, my mother soon understood, was a time when mothers of girls had to be vigilant. Jo of course knew nothing about my crushes, about Rita and me and *The Art of Kissing,* or about the "purity test" all the girls took at camp. The test was actually a list of sexual acts, each worth a numbered score, if you had committed them. Closed-mouth kissing counted one point; open-mouthed, two. Petting above the waist (with clothes on), three. Underneath clothes (what boys called "getting bare hand") was worth five. And so on, up to ten points for going all the way, or sixty-nine, or a blow job, acts which nobody I ever knew admitted to, even in college (where, to my amazement, people were still taking the test; and still lying).

At her friends' urging, my mother began to take an interest, specifically by rounding up acquaintances who could fix me up with blind dates for older kids' parties. She tried her best, and so did I. She provided the party dresses, and the last-minute critical appraisal ("Your hair still needs combing!" or "Is that a pimple?") as I ran to answer the doorbell. I provided the good-night kiss on the bench in the foyer (open-mouthed). Still, not one of the blind dates ever called again.

Then came the fateful grown-up party when she

dressed me up in a Jo Copeland original, right out of her own closet, and sent me off to meet a handsome boy of seventeen, whose very nice (very rich) family owned a big textile mill. This was the kind of boy she had in mind for me. She warned me not to perspire in her beautiful dress, corrected my hair with her own comb, and admonished me to have fun. I never had the slightest idea of what it meant to have fun at a party, much less *how* to have it.

This party was really grown-up—not just spin-the-bottle and post office, but serious necking in very dark corners. As usual, I didn't know anyone, and was far too young (and flat-chested) for anyone to want to know. Plus, there was liquor. I drank two mixed drinks—amber-colored, sweet, with a maraschino cherry—and went to lie down in the host's mother's bedroom, on a pile of coats. I was dimly aware that after a while someone came and sat on the bed, talked to me and held my hand, stroked my face and kissed me. I kept my eyes closed, the way I used to do when I needed my governess to think I was sleeping. After a while, the someone left and I threw up, careful not to let it get on my mother's precious pink and green striped silk.

The following morning, the telephone duly informed Jo of these horrifying events. I was summoned into her bedroom for the most shocking conversation we were ever to have. She was seated on her black velvet ottoman, half naked as usual at this hour, with a towel looped under her breasts. And she was visibly trembling as she shouted what she had just been told. Drunk? Passed out? Boys putting their hands on me? My reputation ruined! *Her* reputation!

I was too stunned to defend myself, even if I had a defense. But I did manage to blurt the only retort I could think of: "Well, I couldn't help it!" At that, she rose from the ottoman and slapped me across the face. Her hand shook less with the force of the slap than with her own terrifying emotion. I had never before seen her whole body shudder, involuntarily, as though *she* had been struck the violent blow.

I hardly felt the slap; certainly it didn't hurt enough to cause tears—which for me was in itself incredible. No waterworks! It was of course the only time in my life she had ever hit me—or, that I could remember, touched me in any way at all. Her nudity somehow made the contact even more startling. Striking me, she was the vulnerable one, more helpless somehow than her punished child.

Years later, when I began to think I understood my mother—or at least knew something of her private terrors—I could finally weep at the memory of that terrible scene. At the revelation of her sudden fear of me, for of course that was what it was. Fear of me as a sexual being. Of my body inside her clothes. My adolescent body, aroused like an animal's, as hers never was. When her hand lashed out at me from her own naked body, it was an impulse as charged as sex itself. There she was, shaken to her core, she who had spent her life seeking refuge from the physical reality of body—birth, sex, passion, death. There she was, after finding her refuge, creating it, in the act of designing clothes. Such a perfection she had achieved; such a beautiful cover-up. Fashion as defense weapon, as bright armorial shield, for a body that must otherwise surely betray her. The art of dressing had to become not only life's work, but ruling passion, in order to be her salvation. Now, here she was, naked, afraid: the physical mother of a physical daughter on the verge of young womanhood.

I fled to my room, sparing us both the agony of another word, or deed.

The son of those nice people did, miraculously, call me up for a date after all. And called again. We dated steadily for months. We went to soda shops for cherry cokes and slow dancing to a jukebox, which was a way to pet standing up. Finally we necked heavily in dark corners of other people's parties. I went up several points on my purity-test score before he graduated from high school and went off to college, where there were girls his own age who would go all the way. I never got up the nerve to ask if he had been the one who kissed me when I was passed out on the coats in his mother's room.

My mother never seemed terribly concerned about any of this. Either because the boy was someone she approved of, or because she had decided to close her eyes in order not to know; in order not to have to do anything. Just as she had done in the days of Fräulein Wegge. Just as I had done, while being kissed in the dark on the pile of coats.

There would never be another confrontation between us over anything to do with sex. I knew it then. I knew it forever when, years later, before I was married, I checked into a hospital for an emergency D & C, necessitated by my bleeding during sex. My mother came to visit and to ask what was wrong with me. I said I had an infection "there." She averted her eyes, stiffened, murmured that I needed to be more careful in cold weather, and she patted me tentatively on the forehead, smoothing my hair. The hand trembled, even at that.

SEEING RED

IT WAS EXPLOSIVE, THE SUDDEN BURST OF REDS THAT BLAZED AROUND US JUST AS RED HERself vanished from my father's life. Gone her pert little tomboy face, her perfect row of Chiclet teeth, the silvery laugh I had mistaken for affection, for warmth, and (dared I imagine) for mother-type love. Gone her son, the boy I thought was my twin, or at least my playmate for keeps, my soul mate for the night train to Florida. We touched tongues when we were three. Impossible that Red could end up choosing husband over life with my dazzling, spirited father; life with me. That she could just disappear, not even whistling good-bye.

Then, as though a switch had been thrown, an extravaganza of Technicolor redheads lit up my lonesome father and me, along with the rest of drab, war-weary America.

Indeed, I thought Technicolor must have been invented for the color red. For the *hair.* Once upon a time, Bette Davis in *Jezebel* had shocked the Old South by wearing red taffeta to a ball, instead of widow's weeds. The world gasped at Bette's scandalous waltz in her swirl of dark, lascivious gray, and somehow believed it saw red.

Now the shock of truer-than-true red was everywhere: Arlene Dahls by the dozen. Rhonda Fleming and fiery Susan Hayward and wisecracker Lucille Ball. Rita Hayworth, pinup girl, putting the blame on Mame. Maureen O'Hara flinging her Titian curls to the sea wind as sexy pirates tied her to the mast. Even men got in on it. Goofball comedy found Red Skelton. Red Barber called the shots in sports. Arthur Godfrey hogged the mike as radio's leading hotshot. Dark, suave William Powell put on a red wig to live *Life with Father,* about a hot-tempered Victorian who sired a whole *tribe* of lovable redheads. Like a herd of wild strawberry roans, they all pranced around as though that hair was a license for being bad. Just as my father's own Red had done, fading away behind her smile, a red Cheshire cat.

Lipstick would soon be wickedly red; all the shades of sin. Nice ladies who once wore Tangee Natural would start painting their luscious mouths in public, bold as scarlet women. Traces of Fire and Ice would be left pointedly on smoldering cigarettes, on the rim of the cocktail glass when they ordered another sloe gin fizz, please, and one more for the road.

I would have to learn about the color, the stain, the "curse" of menstrual blood, with no warning except the nervous giggles of schoolmates who had got theirs first, and boasted that if the pervert flasher leering as we sledded bare-legged downhill in the park ever bothered any of us, *they* could actually have a baby.

Curse or no, my first boyfriend was going all the way at Harvard, and I was still just practicing the Art of Kissing, forbidden red now on my hungry mouth, as blind dates groped me on the bench in the foyer. Soon I tried it in my brother's room; I could throw myself on his bed and at his bored older friends visiting from prep school during their spring vacations. One of those exciting times, Sally would walk in on us and scream: "Open up his pants and crawl in!" My brother would find the three of us locked in that mortifying combat: me and his smirking, red-faced friend, protesting at the top of our guilty lungs; Sally carrying on as though she had caught us red-handed. Going all the way.

And so it was decided: my brother would move out altogether, taking his dangerous friends with him. Our parents' separation agreement had a clause that said, at age sixteen, the boy could choose to live with his father. He used to taunt me with that clause. Now he could go, gleefully, as my father had. And for me it was back to solitary.

How long before my brother would find a redhead of his own? Minutes, it seemed, once he was in my father's orbit. His first serious love interest, a gum-chewer my mother would surely detest, if only for the tight sweater that clashed with the burning bush of her copperwire hair, the Fire and Ice of her mouth. She was two years older than my brother; "experienced." He would see to it that she and Jo never met. On Father's Day he grinned as he came up to collect his mail, saying he was expecting a card from "the twins."

Blissfully unaware of all this "nonsense," my mother was busy redecorating his room; she needed it now for a sort of den, where male visitors could sit in squashy club chairs while knocking back their whiskey, neat. I seldom ventured in there now, except when forced out of my own room to make way for state visits by my mother's important female friends. Carmel would blow in from Beverly Hills and stay for weeks, lolling about in my bed till noon, running Sally's feet off with requests for tea trays, emergency pressing of evening gowns, unpacking bandboxes from the day's shopping. Carmel would also monopolize the phone so that Jo would at last install a second line for herself. It was the least one could do for a star. Though Carmel hadn't been one for years, she never relinquished the aura, or the privileges. Sally never complained. Carmel would after all bring Greer Garson to my mother's parties—and persuade her to wear a Jo Copeland gown when she was voted number one at the box office. I'm not sure what it did for Jo's image later, when Garson married the young actor who had played her son in *Mrs. Miniver.*

Foxy Sondheim would come to stay if her new swain, a handsome gray-templed army major, was in town, and if there were enough swell parties to show him off. Marion Preminger would come home from "darkest Africa" bringing spiritual tidings from Dr. Schweitzer. From south of the border we would get Carmen Lopez y Figueroa, Dolores Del Rio's best friend, who would come bearing spicy tidbits about the vulgar little actress-tart who was just about running Argentina. According to Carmen, Eva Perón forced her friends to shop for her in New York and Paris—"Anything you buy, buy one for me," was the standing order. And Evita never paid them back. Jo Copeland dresses, in duplicate, traveled to Buenos Aires, via Mexico. Carmen paid half-price.

Through Carmen, Jo and Sally also kept track of the growing community of infamous New Yorkers who settled in Mexico like red dust to escape their shady pasts. Any Irishman who got into serious trouble could find a welcome at the Cuernavaca estate of ex-mayor James O'Dwyer. (And half a century later, when Ireland's Bishop Casey fled the scandal over Annie Murphy's American love child, the bishop, too, somehow found his way to Cuernavaca.)

If Carmen or Carmel, Marion or Foxy was in my bed, I would eat and do my homework on the card table in the "den." There were new twin beds in my mother's room; I slept on one of these. They swung apart on a hinge for making up, and then swung back to be rejoined under a huge headboard. Their secret was covered by a voluminous satin spread. Hollow wooden coffins, upholstered like the headboard, hid the pillows by day. Everything about that bed was sleek and hard-edged; the spread was so heavy it took Sally half an hour to smooth it on. But the effect was perfect; just the bed for a desirable woman who resolutely slept alone, yet wanted to convey a more voluptuous impression. We kept very different hours, so my presence in her bed hardly disturbed her.

And while the redecorator was at it, she managed to install a "monkey bar," fitting it cunningly into a closet in the foyer. Playful creatures in red hats and jackets, the costume of an organ grinder's apprentice, scampered mischievously over the walls and peeped around the built-in red leather banquettes. There was a mirrored bar and glass shelves multiplying the images of a remarkable collection of expensive new tumblers, flutes, crushers, zesters, stirrers, swizzle sticks . . .

The pace of parties, the crush of parties, intensified. For one thing, Europe was now coming over here. Refugee artists flocked to New York, making it the world capital of art as well as fashion, lighting up our shiny gray Deco caverns with dots and dashes of red. Mondrian called it jazz, and painted it that way. Pulsing with energy, as if we were all undergoing a transfusion. New blood. Red!

Jo caught the fire almost at once; as the war was ending, fine art suddenly became something one did, like opera and Broadway first nights; like restaurants and the Stork Club. You were seen at galleries, you joined museums and went to members' receptions for the exciting new Roualt show, the Kandinsky, the Klee. Once Jo had gone to the Louvre to marvel at Impressionists. She had seen to it that even I knew how the green shadows illuminated the plump pink flesh of Renoir bathers; how Degas got that incandescent glow in a white ballet tutu. Now Jo was one of the crowd in little black dresses, fetching hair ornaments all aglitter with jet beads and egret plumes. They would troop off to the gallery, and come home with an "important" painting: a charming Picasso gouache of anemones; a cool Milton Avery field whose blue-greens might be light under water. Loveliest of all, inevitably, she would bring home a Kisling portrait of a girl with red hair. She was a wonder, with long eyes the color of melting ice; a long pale luminous throat, and, ah, that burnished, shimmering red-gold glory. Of course I nick-named her Red, but never uttered it aloud in my mother's hearing.

Like all her kind, Kisling's redhead turned out to have a malevolent streak. The week she arrived, I met my Uncle Eddie by chance on a midtown street corner. It was snowing heavily; he was in rolled-up shirtsleeves, bare-headed, strolling along Lexington Avenue, munching on a shiny red apple. It was just the sort of poison apple the evil queen (wearing Fire and Ice lipstick) offered to Snow White. Uncle Eddie seemed more than usually strange that day; as always, he gave no sign that he knew what was happening all around him. The scurrying, buttoned-up crowds, the swirling white flakes, the biting wind, his own bare head and arms, the bright red fruit. He barely recognized me; we only nodded hello.

Uncle Eddie died the following day. Of insulin shock, I was eventually told, though I didn't comprehend that. Eddie had been a diabetic; he must have forgotten to take his injection that day of the blizzard. Or else he took too much. Or else he bit the evil queen's poison apple.

For weeks my mother was sick with grief. No matter that Eddie had caused her to make disastrous mistakes all her life. No matter that he had twice guided her to the brink of financial ruin; that but for him she would have been rich, that they had always fought like sworn enemies, slamming down the phone on each other's screams, then not speaking for months at a time. Eddie was the only son of both her father and her mother. Minna's only boy; Jo's only true blood brother.

I never dared tell my mother that I blamed his death on the Kisling redhead. The ice-water eyes of the portrait now seemed to follow me, like that accusing gaze in those eerie portraits of Jesus in His crown of thorns. I had loved Red; it was a betrayal of my mother. Kisling's redhead must have known.

And when she, too, disappeared—my mother sold her at a healthy profit, never suspecting how much I cared—I raged at the loss, as if she were the original.

The surprise was that I mourned the original longer than my father did. He would soon be seen around town with another "gal," as his friends would say. This one's name was Edna, so he called her "little Ed," a diminutive of his own name. It was, for the moment, close enough to "Red." At least it rhymed. Unfortunately the affair with little Ed, a brunette, came to a bad end when he took her along on that winter's Florida vacation (I was no longer invited). She would be paying her own way. But as he recounted it, they had a terrific row the night they arrived. Over sex, was what he implied, though I suspected it might have been over her refusal to tint her hair the required shade. In any case, little Ed walked out of the hotel room—and his life—taking the best three coat hangers in the closet.

After that, he never seemed to date anyone who wasn't a redhead, true or false. The irony of it struck me years later. My father was congenitally colorblind. He was forever cursing the makers of golf tees for coloring them red and thus rendering them, to him, invisible in the grass. The truth was that he had never seen Red at all.

NEW YORK'S CHARACTER HAD ALWAYS
SEEMED SET IN STONE — SOME OF IT PRECIOUS, LIKE
the pavement that sparkled under streetlights, suggesting
buried treasure. Now they began tearing it up, tearing it
down, like frenzied football fans attacking the goalposts
after the big game. In the euphoria of war's happy ending, of victory, streets brimming with homecoming boys
kissing hometown girls, of cheers and tears and confetti
streamers, there was no time for a moment of silence, a
pause for reflection. We were in this tearing hurry to get
past the frightening question: we won; now what?

If the skyline was the limit, New York would get
higher. And somehow it would grow colder too. When
the jackhammers ceased, we had grand new ice palaces,
rows of smooth-skinned glass buildings staring rudely at

each other, seeing only reflections of their own blank gaze. It was an eerie foreshadowing of the time to come when we, too, would hide behind mirrored shades, protecting ourselves from the danger of being seen through by passing strangers.

Herb came home with the other heroes; a captain cited by General MacArthur, sporting medals and his old irresistible grin. Sally had forbidden him to marry the girl he had met and loved in Australia; he was to come right home and fulfill his mother's American dream — marrying someone she approved of, having a nice family and a good job, a house in the suburbs with a den and a dinette. He would not move back into his old room behind my mother's kitchen. He would not wait there for me to grow up.

The week he came back, as bidden, Sally cornered my Uncle Abbott in my mother's dining room. Before she would serve him his soup, she exacted the promise of a job for her son in Abbott's big textile firm. It was the least my family could do. So my hero did not come back to me; he returned to work, to night school on the GI bill, to a future in a gray flannel suit, to the altar with a girl that passed Sally's muster, and to Sally herself. She was still writing all our scripts.

My family's world, like the century itself, suddenly seemed to be racing toward — and fleeing from — middle age. New York's new look reflected that crisis as much as anything. Reinventing its own shiny, youthful image, proving itself still vigorous, still electric. We were already inhabiting the futuristic fantasy that the World's Fair, only a few years before, called Tomorrowland.

The sheer towers rising around us were starkly beautiful, like sculpture; glass and steel birds in flight. The United Nations headquarters soared over the East River like an upright vitrine in a great department store, displaying the fragile promise of world peace. So many flags flying on glittering masts, such a brave trooping of colors in the fresh breeze over the new ribbon of highway that hemmed the island. Wishful semaphores for a future in glass houses, where no one would dare cast the first stone.

For a while, I would scarcely notice what was happening in the streets of Manhattan. No sooner was I allowed to cross them alone, than I couldn't wait to escape them. If Herb wasn't going to rescue me after all, if I was too big to think I could run away with three weeks' allowance, then I must find another exit. The Upper East Side had a rarefied airlessness; it could hold you for life, breathing shallowly. My prison was still bounded by Lexington Avenue and Central Park; by home, school, social dancing class. By my family's expectations that I would grow up, marry and die there, and count my cell bars as blessings.

One day I found myself staring at the entrance to the IRT subway station outside my school. There it was; I could use it to burrow out underground. Faster than a speeding bullet, and only a nickel ride, into real worlds that were another part of New York. My mother had never descended those forbidding steps, never learned the arcane language of getting from here to there in a tunnel. I hadn't done it either, but I knew I must. Never since her Brooklyn childhood had Jo traveled to another borough. The world, yes, but never Queens, never the Bronx. I could start there. Exotic planets, all within reach.

The children of my mother's friends were by now safely tucked away out of town—in prep schools, military academies, boarding schools or, if they were still here, in a good private school close to home. Nearly all my Hunter classmates whose families could afford it would soon disperse to those same destinations. I asked about boarding school; indeed, I begged. With my brother's prep school already costing the earth, I was told, it was out of the question. I suspected that the real reason was the scandal about my cousin Wendy, who had been sent to a modest Quaker boarding school where she had danced with "colored boys" and fallen in love with one. "Poor Aunt Billie," as my mother put it, went through a nightmare to get her daughter out, and lost a year's tuition. I had better resign myself to a nice, affordable private school, within walking distance.

So I came up with the answer. There were elite public high schools scattered around the city—subway rides away. Academic excellence, and no tuition. Free, except for the nickel fare. High School of Music and Art. Brooklyn Tech. Bronx High School of Science. My father had gone to a public high school. My mother was happy to save the money. If I could qualify, I could go. *Free.*

I was already planning to do my homework on those interminable subway rides; planning to put on lipstick and stare boldly at boys who didn't go to social dancing class on the Upper East Side. Unsuitable boys. Badly dressed grown-ups hanging from straps, whizzing through unfamiliar territory. The real world.

All I had to do was skip another grade and pass a qualifying test to prove scientific aptitude (not Music and Art, I decided; art belonged to my mother). I chose Bronx Science. Though I had not the slightest interest in science, I had a keen interest in Bronx Science's ratio of boys to girls: roughly twenty to one. Amazingly, no one ever questioned my motives, not when I applied ("She's going *where?*" shrieked my Aunt Mildred, but that was all); not after I got in and my grades began plummeting from straight-A to disgraceful; not even when I got an unprecedented C for my independent biology project, which demanded that I pull the wings off three dozen generations of hapless fruit flies, to prove that an acquired trait—such as a passion for dressing up—could not be inherited.

My social life also failed to improve. My mother assumed this was caused by Sloppy Joe sweaters and dirty saddle shoes, rather than the fact that the school was populated entirely by greasy-grind poor kids killing themselves to get into MIT. And that as usual I was much too young and flat-chested to distract them—even from Mechanical Drawing.

Jo could not have helped me then, even if she had understood. She was once again busy making fashion history. Her own ideas never seemed to falter—not with the wartime silhouette; not now, when others curtsied to the postwar "New Look" as Paris got back in the act. The press crowned Christian Dior king of postwar fashion for his nipped-in waist and long full skirt: the "return to femininity," as they called it, signaling American women that it was time to quit their jobs and get back to the kitchen. Early television showed them the way: smiling wives in shirtwaist dresses, puffed out with crinoline petticoats, cooking up one-dish casserole suppers in their gleaming new (servantless) kitchens. Avocado and Harvest Gold refrigerators! For nostalgia, there was Loretta Young as a TV hostess, twirling in a sumptuous hostess gown like a glamorous relic of some prehistoric America.

Jo Copeland went on doing what she had always done: dressing women with exciting lives outside the home—day and night. Watching her, studying her clothes, you would never know there had been a war on, or that it had ended, or that women's lives would be changed again for another generation. When they finally emerged in the late 1960s, she would still be there for them, with a slinky dinner suit, a grand evening gown; with masterly detail, luxurious fabrics and trimming, and the wit that could line a tweed suit with brilliant yellow silk, so you could flash it, or fling it back over your chair and dazzle everyone sitting behind you. She could paint peacock feathers on organdie, or scatter ostrich fronds in red bugle beads over a red crepe gown, and make the high drama seem like a force of nature.

In the postwar years, only a handful of U.S. designers were making ready-to-wear that was recognized as couture caliber. She was one of these, whose work actually scooped Paris with what came to be called "prêt-à-porter." So good was the workmanship by now, and so huge the market, that even Dior began designing a

French line expressly for American women — to be made in New York. The tide had turned.

Jo had once been called the Chanel of America. By the middle of the century she was not, and had no need to be, compared to anyone.

ENSEMBLE III

WHEN THE DREADED BOX ARRIVED, TWICE
PER SEMESTER, I WOULD SLIDE IT UNDER MY BED
and wait for Pamela's visit. She would always come
promptly. Pamela was not really a friend; in fact I had no
use for her other than this one. She was simply the pretti-
est girl I knew: tall, model-slim, blond, creamy—a perfect
specimen by my mother's lights. Unlike most of my dis-
reputable, unwashed-jeans-clad dorm-mates at Wellesley,
Pamela never sat around scarfing brownies with fudge
sauce, arguing about Nietzsche, taking the purity test or
mocking the girls with circle pins and twinsets whose
four-year college agendas were set before they arrived:
1) Harvard freshman mixer; 2) Select Harvard man;
3) Engagement ring by graduation; 4) Marriage six months
later.

Pamela would have been one of those if she'd gone to Wellesley. But she went to a junior college down the road, for post-debs who only needed a two-year rest-stop between the coming-out party and the big society wedding. The thing was, Pamela loved Jo Copeland dresses; she was the only girl I ever met who did. Jo didn't design for girls; that was at least one good reason for my looking so awful in her creations. Not the only one, granted.

After the first time, Pamela's visits became part of my core curriculum; a required freshman course. She would come for half an hour, let me bore her with my deepest thoughts about Plato and the Epicureans while she tried on the contents of the box, modeling each carefully chosen number that my mother thought I must need for football weekends and dinner dates in Boston. Never once did I disabuse her, or let her suspect that I wore nothing but those jeans and a surplus Navy pea coat; that I never went anywhere but the campus hangout, for the brownies and the bull sessions about philosophy and sex.

At the end of the visit, Pamela would pack up the clothes in their tissue sandwiches and take the box away. I never asked whether or where she wore the stuff; perhaps she sold it or traded for tutoring in art appreciation. But the visit was important to me. It got rid of the box; it enabled me to talk convincingly while thanking my mother on the phone: Oh, I love the yellow bolero with the chalk and jet beads; I can't wait to wear the iridescent green taffeta; I was worried about the low neckline but it's perfect; I look like a flower on a stalk.

The cruelty of what I was doing never occurred to me. A form of matricide, really.

It was surely a more devious, more potent rebellion than my daring to invite a black classmate home for spring break. My friend Gladys was light-skinned and pretty, but my mother heard she was "colored" after the night doorman mentioned it to Sally. How could you do such a thing? she raged. Nearly as apoplectic as she had been the time she slapped me for passing out drunk in her lovely striped silk dress. The crime was the same, of course; causing talk about *her*.

After Gladys, she summoned my father for a conference about what to do with me; perhaps I was turning pinko; perhaps I should be transferred to some less radical girls' school, preferably back in New York, where I could be watched. By whom, they didn't specify. I said if I was to be transferred, I'd choose Radcliffe, where at least they didn't teach you how to pour tea, and where they wouldn't consider their most distinguished alumna to be the woman who married Chiang Kai-shek. My father's eyes rolled at that, as if I'd blasphemed. What corporate leader, what head of state, he wanted to know, would be caught dead dating a dog from Radcliffe—let alone marrying one?

In the end I went back to Wellesley, with a warning. And they would do what had to be done to curb my "tendencies." More blind dates. Charm school in the summer. Another box of clothes. When Pamela left junior college to get married, I had no choice but to gain forty pounds. That stopped the boxes.

PATTULLO-JO COPELAND

SEPARATES IV

CAPTIVES OF THE COLD WAR, WE LEARNED
FAST ABOUT JUMPING AT OUR SHADOWS. SPIES
lurked, and ring around the collar, and old pals who
might have been pinkos all along. What if you were spot-
ted driving last year's car? What if you didn't have tail fins
and white shortie gloves? Did the rumpus room paneling
wipe clean with a damp cloth? Did you really do-it-your-
self? Maybe *you* were un-American. It would take more
than another decade before the word "plastic" turned
into an epithet for everything phony and disposable, including our most fervent fifties ideas.

Getting married in the fifties was as contagious as the
new Golden Rule. When the H-bomb fell, we were advised, if desperate neighbors showed up at the fallout
shelter door, you'd better shoot. The logic seemed unas-

sailable: you'd have stocked just enough canned tuna and breathable air for your family. And the folks at the door should have built their own.

Fear of not being safely married in that dangerous time was hardly limited to the huddled masses of bright young college grads let loose in the teeming city, hanging on to their virginity and their typing speed, yearning to give them both up for Mr. Right.

My mother's women friends, career divorcées, were suddenly slipping into second and third marriages as though into next season's navy-blue suit. Foxy did it. Carmel Myers, after a brief widowhood, did it too. Even my Aunt Billie inexplicably said yes to the funny little man she had been brushing off since I was eight. But now Elmer sold insurance—million-dollar policies—and wrote a how-to guide called *The Sale Begins When the Customer Says No*, a bestseller in fifteen languages. The family joke was that it took Elmer eleven years to sell himself to Billie.

But when Jo succumbed to the strange new virus, everyone was genuinely shocked. One minute she was flitting from sample-room floor to zebra banquette, Paris, the Riviera. Buying her own first mink, "blowing" herself (as she always put it) to diamond earrings from Harry Winston. The next minute she was madly in love. My mother, blushing and clinging, gazing adoringly at some guy in a crew cut and a Brooks Brothers suit. It was a sight I never thought I'd see.

Mitch met Jo's strictest standards and, I must say, most of mine. Tall and sexy, smart and charming, with a sly sense of irony and a faint air of mystery (where had he been all our lives?), he even had a fifties kind of job: network executive—so he could do exciting things like persuading Margaret Truman to host a talk show. He was too good not to have been married before—nobody ever found out how many times—but he had emerged unscathed, meaning without alimony or child support. Best of all, he looked terrific in evening clothes, and didn't seem to mind wearing them every night. Nor did he tire of telling Jo that she looked terrific too. You could almost hear her purr.

He didn't quite meet Sally's standards, however. While he was a sight more dashing than her previous choice, the faithful Philippe, and several escorts since (not counting my father, still the sentimental favorite), the fact was that Mitch didn't seem to have much beyond his looks, his job and his white tie. He lived in a fifth-floor walkup bachelor pad on East Fifty-eighth Street (near but not *on* Sutton Place), which no one recalled having seen. "Walk up?" Jo would murmur, uncomprehending. Once he'd popped the question, and she'd said yes, he agreed to get rid of the pad. In fact he offered it to me. I had just landed my first real job—reporter on a Queens newspaper—so I could pay the rent. And since he had hung onto the place through all his previous lives, my mother took this sacrifice as a good omen for their future. They could do over my room as a den. The hateful cabbage roses would be gone at last. And so would I.

Jo and Mitch had what then passed for a prenuptial agreement—a crude pact by today's lights. They would live on his salary. That is, he would pay the landlord, Sally and the food and liquor bills. Jo would spring for

the extras. It sounded okay to Sally; she gave her bless-
ing.

My father and I were dancing at my mother's wedding.
She was looking at us, critically, over the shoulder of her
new bridegroom. It was whispered that Mitch had a
drinking problem; that he had been married four times
before, not twice, as he claimed; that he was bisexual; a
fortune hunter, and five years younger than the age he
declared on the marriage license. None of it seemed to
bother Jo.

My father was still just as handsome as Mitch; a different type. Mitch was a mix of Louis Calhern and Fred
MacMurray. Craggy; suave; possibly a crook; engaging.
But strangers still came up to my father and told him he
could be Cary Grant's double. They had both aged mag-
nificently. And though my father no longer struck his
chin with the straight of his hand, to develop a Cary
Grant cleft, he did use Ever-Youth to darken his chest
hair.

We were dancing in the square mirrored foyer of my
mother's apartment. The mirrors had been recently
installed; behind them lay a series of other dancing figures, those huge painted Harlequins and Columbines. In
this decade, in my mother's world, Harlequins were now
passé. Like being single. Mirrors were mounted everywhere, pressing against the fanciful masked, dancing
lovers. Now we were dancing before the mirrors, mirror-
ing the movements of those invisible ghosts hidden in the

walls. My father and I circled my mother and her bride-groom. She was wearing pale gray, fawn, pearl. Her shoes gleamed as she pranced; the handsome Mitch had pale eyes, dove-gray hair at his temples; hair cut short, bris-tling, a military brush. My father's hair was still black, smooth as Cary Grant's. I studied my reflection, as though it wasn't me. Who was that girl dancing with Cary Grant? Such a heavy, awkward girl, with a head that ducked forward on her neck as though it had been snapped. She was out of step with the music, stepping on her partner's nimble feet. Cary Grant seemed not to no-tice; he was engrossed in the moving picture of his ex-wife and her sudden husband. They looked wonderful together. My father was noticing that Mitch was equally handsome in his different way, and perhaps two inches taller than my father. Did he feel jealousy, anger, regret? My mother had not been his wife for eighteen years. He had left her, us, whistling.

Two weeks after this wedding, my father took his yearly vacation in Florida, found a new lady friend, and married her within ten days. A whirlwind courtship, a dance. She was half his age, slim, blonde (not red), a mother of two young children, a boy and a girl. She had a deep Southern accent, and wore boys' button-down shirts, barrettes in her hair. Rumors flew about her, just as they did about Mitch. Indeed, many of them were the same rumors: that she had been married four times be-fore, not twice, as she claimed—and that, just like Mitch, she was a fortune hunter. Her name was Nancy; she pro-nounced it in three syllables: Nay-un-cy.

I thought it was significant that my father never persuaded Nay-un-cy to dye her hair red. I never dared ask either of them whether he had tried.

If Nay-un-cy was indeed a fortune-hunter, she had miscalculated badly this time. My father had done the same, for in Florida Nay-un-cy had given him the distinct impression that she was a North Carolina belle; that the second of her two husbands had died suddenly during their honeymoon, leaving her both pregnant and extremely rich.

Most of this, my father slowly learned, was a Southern regional fiction (doubly ironic in its near-match to my mother's mystery romance). Nevertheless, Nay-un-cy insisted on the large, expensive Sutton Place apartment, the North Carolina bric-a-brac. My father borrowed a great deal of money, bought Nay-un-cy what she wanted, and tried to enjoy married life as the proud father of a new, readymade family: a boy and a girl. Ironic, as my brother said to me. I said nothing. Within a year, after Nay-un-cy and my father had ceased to speak to each other, he bought her the last expensive luxury: divorce. My mother's parting from the handsome, mysterious Mitch cost her dearly too, though in another currency. It occurred to me, much later, that though Jo and Ed should perhaps never have married, they should also never have married anyone else. That in some unknowable sense, he did possess her—and she, him—after all.

Technically the marriage of Jo and Mitch lasted four years, but it was all over, bar the shouting, in less than a month. Almost as soon as Jo had exorcised my childhood from her new husband's den—substituting dark blue walls and gentlemen's-club seating for my chintz and the doll shelves—than Mitch began to hide out in there with his books, scotch and a stack of *Christian Science Monitor*s. The tux and the dancing shoes refused to budge from his cedar-lined closet (formerly my prison, my vault). He simply retired from active duty.

It turned out that he had a legitimate grievance, which he made no attempt to keep secret. The bride refused to share her bed. Refused! Could you beat that? And the subject had never come up till after the wedding. Her lifelong "white marriage" dream; she forgot to tell him.

He retaliated with cruel and unusual punishment, just as my father had. Telling me about it, for one thing. Making a pass at me, and then at my roommate. At least my father complained behind Jo's back ("I never possessed that woman"), but Mitch chose full frontal attack. He would roll his eyes when she didn't get his jokes, or when his smart repartee went over her head, as he meant it to. "My bride," he would sigh, "isn't quite with us, I'm afraid."

There would be sly winks across the table if she had anything serious to say. He ridiculed her taste, her habits, her friends, her choices in night spots—the very things he had professed to find so delightful. How could she fall asleep at the opera, arrive late everywhere, change her clothes five times a day at a weekend house party, never read a book . . .

Soon he began to drink in earnest, as a matter of

principle, with the door locked. He went to church to atone, and out with other women to compensate.

I knew it wasn't fair; it was rotten. Yet I sided with him; I pitied him; I identified with him. How could she? And if she could, how could she not know what would happen? She was still, resolutely, all dressed up with someplace to go. She had tempted a worse fate than that of a single woman shopping for escorts in an age of couples. For she was coupled, yet shamefully alone.

It probably wasn't a coincidence that my father's bizarrely hasty marriage also began to fall apart soon after it started. Nancy, his embarrassingly young Southern comfort, had forced him to move from his gloomy hotel flat to a sumptuous co-op on (not *near*) Sutton Place. She had imported a North Carolina decorator to "do it up" in pastels and "window treatments," ruffled swags and Austrian shades. Despite her supposed independent means as a rich widow, all the bills had gone to my father. So did the private-school tuitions for her son and daughter, and, for the boy, membership in the Knickerbocker Grays, an elite military afterschool program featuring drills and West Point–style uniforms.

My brother—by now grown up, married and single-handedly saving the family business for my father—watched in horror when Nancy's nine-year-old boy came to visit the office, where my father introduced him as "my son, the future cigar manufacturer."

Reactions were swift and predictable: my brother accepted a hostile takeover bid from a bigger tobacco company, and sold the family business out from under the family. It was a brilliant maneuver; everyone made a handsome profit; my brother became a tycoon; my father was forced out of his presidency into a golden handshake and a five-year contract as a "consultant." (No one ever consulted him again.) There was bad blood everywhere for a very long time, but Nay-un-cy's boy would never again set foot in the office.

Soon after that, my father and Nancy stopped speaking; they stayed in separate rooms, kept separate hours and lived separate lives together on Sutton Place. When he finally divorced her, sold the co-op, agreed to the ruinous alimony, he moved into a new gloomy bachelor flat about two blocks away from the old one.

Jo and Mitch didn't actually call it quits until the building I had grown up in went co-op. She bought our apartment cheap and sold it fast, for an impressive sum — enough to move into a new life. As she saw it, Park Avenue and the Upper East Side were passé. She wanted a sixties kind of setting, a "with-it" little penthouse in one of the new midtown high-rises. She found just the thing: four rooms instead of eight; two narrow slivers of terrace, and a kitchen smaller than her old hall closet. Also, there was no suite behind the kitchen for Sally and her salon. There was in fact no room for either a Sally or a Mitch. And when Jo moved, they both left her. At the time she had no idea that, of the two, Sally would prove the more wrenching loss. Years later, after a succession of household day workers, my mother called me to complain that her maid of the moment had been ill for several days, and the wastepaper baskets were full. What, she asked, should she do?

As patiently as possible, I tried to explain how one

might find a little door just down the hall, discreetly marked INCINERATOR, and on it one might discover a handle. If she would pull it toward her, she could tip the wastepaper into a sort of drawer, and it would go away. My mother thanked me, and I gave it no further thought for several days. Then I called her to ask how she was, and whether she had emptied the wastebaskets. Yes, she said brightly; she had solved the problem. I should have known better than to ask how, but I did, and she told me. She had pressed the elevator button, and when the man came up, she had given him five dollars to take away the full baskets and bring them back empty.

My mother never did learn to keep house, carry groceries, or love anyone. Like the protective mother who had died for Jo, Sally had seen to it that Jo never needed to know the facts of ordinary life. I had to acknowledge that theirs was the closest thing to a true partnership either of them had ever achieved. A white marriage, of sorts. But after all, it too was bound to have an unhappy ending.

MODELS II

YEARS LATER, WHEN I WROTE MY FIRST NOVEL, *SUCH GOOD FRIENDS*, MY MOTHER MET THE fictional daughter, unhappy and not too well groomed, of a chic, unsympathetic mother. Jo's friends began calling her as soon as the book came out, to commiserate, to snicker, to quote Shakespeare on the serpent's tooth and the thankless child. To make matters worse, the book was published just as Jo's career ended; Pattullo had closed its doors that spring.

I tried to alleviate the hurt, or at least my part of it, by explaining that fiction was not literal truth, that I loved my mother, that she was not the model for the monster in my book. I meant it, to my own surprise, but she was not consoled.

The fact was, she was defenseless at La Côte Basque,

and in her friends' living rooms. It was as if I'd undressed her in public. But then the novel became a success: foreign editions, film rights, bestsellerdom. People who impressed my mother were impressed.

Jo flung her silver-fox scarf over her shoulder and met her friends at La Côte Basque, just so that she could boast: "Guess who's playing me in my daughter's movie? Nina Foch!"

The characters in the film had one exchange that made me wince with remembered pain. The grieving heroine, her husband dying, her marriage shattered by news of his adulteries, turns to her mother for warmth, for comfort. The mother suggests she do something about her hair, her clothes, maybe have a facial and a pedicure. The daughter looks stricken, the mother looks helpless. "It's all I know," she sighs.

I didn't see the movie with my mother, but she did see it. And she said Nina Foch looked very smart. I had to smile.

If you didn't have your family, what would you write? my father had asked me once. Not a pleasant question. What would any writer write? I retorted, trying not to squirm. He was embarrassed by me; I had embarrassed him! Has anyone actually finished reading this book of yours? he demanded then. He had ploughed through some forty pages. He had telephoned several times over two weeks, reporting his painful progress. Then he had stopped trying. Did he mean to make me feel this bad?

Some people, I said, have read it, have even liked it. Not many, though, I admitted. He shrugged, irritated.

The last one you wrote was filth; this one is just boring. This one is just a disgrace to the family.

I'm sorry, I murmured, flinching. A sorry response for a grown woman, a published writer, a person with children of her own. None of which counted. Only the wild storm of baby emotions he had struck with his thunderbolt of displeasure. It was not even anger; only that cold censure I had so coveted each time he came to punish my brother. Coveted! Could anyone but my father ever cause my throat to close with such terror and desire? How I had craved the look on his face when he arrived, summoned by my distraught mother, to administer the formal beating of his son for some grave misdeed, some failure at school, some fresh torment of me. All I ever wished then was for my sins to count, my failures to deserve the belt, the hairbrush, the closed door, the howling screams. The whistling sound of the descending weapon, and the other sound, the sickening smack as buckle sliced into flesh. How I had begged my father for it, hit *me,* not him! Me! And how they misunderstood, all of them. They thought I meant to defend my brother. I only wanted my father's wrath, which I mistook for love. And now I had won it. And there was no mistake: not love.

Jo actually threw me a publication party for my second book. This time no one taunted her about a character that bore some resemblance to her. Even though there was one, she didn't recognize it. That book, too, was a success; a newspaper photographed us together, mother and daughter, under the headline "Such Good Friends."

She wore one of my very favorite Jo Copeland originals: black taffeta with a full skirt of pleated ruffles, lace collar and cuffs dazzling with French crystal. I called it her "fortunate Pilgrim" dress; deservedly one of the bestsellers of her long designing life. I was wearing a floor-length cardigan sweater, sexy, with side slits thigh-high. For the first time ever, I heard her say she liked how I looked, that I had discovered my own style, that I'd inherited something after all.

At the party she gave for me, someone said she must be very proud of her brilliant daughter, and she said yes, though I knew she didn't understand what they meant by "proud," or "brilliant." Just as I had not understood, all those years ago, when I first saw a showing of her beautiful designs.

We had come full circle.

ONE DAY MY FATHER DECIDED TO DIE; HE
WOULD DO NOTHING TO HASTEN DEATH, BUT HE
would be orderly, his things packed; he would not be
taken by surprise. I visited him in his sad brown apartment. (I finally understood why, colorblind, he had
always chosen brown, believing it to be a pleasing gray-
green, the color of morning in the country, of mist on a
golf-club fairway.) He now kept the television set tuned to
a channel that listed stock prices, rolling lines of hiero-
glyphics. There was no sound. He had very little money
now, but he had a history of owning stocks, and he continued to live there, in that time. The largest brown chair
was set squarely in front of the television screen. An old
alarm clock, ticking, was placed on top of the set. He was
in his "office," engaged in important matters. He picked

his nose absently; when I was a child I hated seeing him do this; he did it in darkened movie theaters, or at home, behind his newspaper. It seemed to me then that he only ceased to do it during meals, while smoking his cigar, playing golf, or beating my brother. Now he no longer smoked; he had had a pacemaker implanted in his chest. The outlines of it were visible through his skin; as though he had ingested a Walkman.

He was wearing striped pajamas, a robe and gleaming leather slippers, a gift from one of the last lady friends. Even now, my father was never at a loss for lady friends. He still made them all dye their hair red, so he could still call them Red, the nickname of his first, his truest love, the redhead he was with on the night my dark-haired mother gave birth to me.

He looked up as I came in, nodded and smiled, turned back to the screen. Numbers were rolling. He could not speak while numbers were rolling. I was disturbing him at work.

The nurse, a grim black woman, clattered in the kitchenette preparing his lunch. The clock on the TV indicated that it was lunchtime. My father beckoned me to the sofa opposite his chair, leaned toward me conspiratorially, without taking his eyes from the rolling numbers. I'm going to fire this one too, he said. His tone was gleeful. I nodded, implying sympathy, approval, assent. He still had a need to fire people, even if they were only women. So long as a man can get rid of a woman, he would say, he is still free, he is still a man.

The nurse confided that he would not use the bedpan, although it had become quite difficult for him to manage the trip to the bathroom without an accident. She did not understand that a bedpan was not an acceptable object for the office of an important businessman. It smacked of infancy, of helplessness, of women in control of one's private life. As long as he lived, my father would go to the bathroom like a businessman.

When he'd had the pacemaker installed, his doctor advised him to avoid undue excitement. My father immediately gave up bridge, which he loved, and his current lady friend, whom he did not love. Following the stock market on TV was not up for renouncing. That was business.

Dad? I said, after a respectful interval. Mm? he replied, picking his nose, watching the rolling numbers.

Those are nice slippers, I said.

Red gave them to me, he said. Can't stand that woman.

The nurse brought his lunch tray and set it on the table. He would have to relinquish his seat on the exchange.

I handed him his cane, and helped him rise out of the brown chair. He seemed so fragile, my father. He was not even small, not even old.

This egg is too soft, he shouted. *Two* minutes; *two*. The nurse set her mouth in a thin line. My father looked at me, triumphant in his rage. You see? he said. They can't even count! None of 'em can count!

I exchanged a glance of sympathy with the woman; quick flicker of the eye, all I dared.

I watched him eat his egg, his spoonful of cottage cheese. A sudden memory of him eating an enormous bowl of some wonderful creamy stuff, mysterious. Little flecks of red-edged transparent discs peeped from it. I thought it must be dessert, a snowy mountain of sweetness, a fairy-tale food. I begged for a taste. He held his spoon to my mouth, pushed it in; I found myself invaded by sour lumps of wet chalk. Gagging, retching, vomiting on the polished table. How could he betray me, my father? He rose, shouting, furious, his lunch spoiled. Someone came to clean the mess, someone came to take me away. Sobbing. Cottage cheese, sour cream, radishes. I was barely two years old.

Now, here, it was time for his nap. I went to sit beside the bed for a moment, like a hospital visitor. The nurse smoothed his covers, fussed with the pillow. He growled at her to get away, to leave him alone. He folded his hands neatly on the taut sheet over his sunken belly. His fingernails were very clean; I remembered that he used to have a manicurist come to his office. Businessmen did that. Their buffed nails shone like their polished shoes. They had soft dark coats, homburgs. They hid behind newspapers.

Dad? I said.

Women, he said, exhaling the word like bad air.

I'll come back later, I said, rising to kiss him. He did not unclasp his hands; they had been placed exactly where he wanted them. The nap would last forty minutes; then he had to get back to work.

Everything is in order, he said, as I bent over him.

Yes, I said.

•

I remembered when, after my grandfather's funeral, my father had ordered the moving men to take everything away from his suddenly impoverished mother. All those tapestries, Belgian linens, diamonds, chokers, tiaras and opera capes. My father was the one who had to empty her life. The servants, and the Packard limousine, Harold the chauffeur and his livery. I remembered how old my grandmother suddenly looked, like a very old woman. She was only fifty-six, but her life had ended. I remembered my father supervising the removal of her things, and then of her, and of his youngest brother, who had never married, and who still lived with her. My father moving them both into a stark two-room efficiency unit in a small residential hotel, almost exactly like his own, in another part of town. My grandmother never smiled again. I still have the photograph of her sitting in her high-backed chair in that severe little efficiency unit. A framed photograph of my grandfather—she still called him Dearie—conspicuously displayed beside her. He's wearing his gold watch chain, stretched across the ample belly I remember; the German badge of good living; of success.

One by one as the uncles died, my father continued to pay off his father's debts—to his widowed aunts, to his cousins. Women, he would say to me; *women.* Such a hateful word. I had vowed never to be one. It was odd that he never spoke ill of his reckless, dishonorable crook of a father. It was odd that I didn't find it odd. *Women* bled the business dry; that was his lifelong burden. I understood.

Somehow I had always assumed my poor father was

also burdened by me, and my brother. That my mother supported us entirely out of her earnings was kept a shameful secret, by him, and even by her. She would not have it known that she was such a failure. For as she saw it, any woman whose husband leaves her to fend for herself is a failure. If she must fend for children too, she is a drudge, a lower-class person, an outcast. It was one thing to be famous and talented, to travel and dress elegantly, on the fruits of one's talent. It was quite another thing, an unmentionable thing, to work because one needed money, in order to live. That was why I went to public schools expensively dressed, and had a governess till I was twelve, unlike anyone else in my school, or indeed anywhere. Among my classmates were some whose mothers "had to work," whose grandmothers came to pick them up after school. My mother was different; it was never said that she "worked." She was a designer, something like a movie star. Where she went all day, what she did in those beautiful clothes of hers, was not explained. To me, she was not a working mother; she was a mystery. It never occurs to children that parents don't choose the way they are.

I saw my father once more. Lying in the same position, hands folded neatly over the neat, tight covers. Dad?

Women ruined the business, he said. Women and their drapes.

How, Dad? How did they do it?

They couldn't stand the smell of cigars, he sighed. His eyes were closed. I tiptoed out. The nurse—he had not managed to fire this one after all—shook her head. I didn't ask what she meant by this gesture; I already knew I had heard my father's last words.

The task of clearing his life away fell to me and my sister-in-law. My brother was busy; another businessman. There was little of value among the brown things. A watch, an elegant old watch, white gold, not his taste, probably a gift from my mother. What shall we do with this? my sister-in-law asked, holding it aloft. I'll take it, I said, surprising us both. And the silk pocket scarves.

Those nurses must have cleaned him out, my brother said. Where were all the cufflinks, the studs? All the gifts from all the redheads, true and false?

My brother and I went to the funeral home together. My father, I said to the rabbi, was a wonderfully handsome man. It was his pride, if not his joy.

Saw action, my father wrote, in a note that he had composed for his own obituary. *Saw action in World War I.*

A wonderfully handsome man, said the rabbi at the service. My mother nodded. Three redheaded women nodded. It was a good service.

A woman is on trial for child abuse; her daughter is dead, a suicide. The charge is that the mother forced the girl to dance naked in a bar, and used the money she earned to help support them both. The girl presumably killed herself out of shame, or despair. Blame-the-mother. My father taught me how. Who else was there to blame, after all? The father? My father? God, the father? An absurd notion. Father knows best, father does his best, father is a busy man, a businessman.

He said he never "possessed" my mother. Never possessed that woman, he told me. I didn't understand, of course. I was only seven or eight. But I knew she had failed him, hadn't loved him, hadn't wanted me, or my brother, didn't love any of us. Didn't even have a secretary to write to us, affectionately.

But he was the one who left, whistling.

In the Great Depression, it is now admitted, many fathers left. One in five or one in four. Divorce was only for fathers who could afford lawyers; poorer ones just left. My father, I learned, years later, left differently from the way my cousin's father had, or Sally's husband, Herb's father. Different too, I imagine, from the father of the dead girl whose mother is on trial.

At least my father came to visit, though he didn't help pay our bills. All those Friday night visits, which he called our "dates." He and I eating in the dining room, like a couple, while my mother went out with *her* dates. The only times I ate in that room, or ate with any company at all, were those times my father came. My nurse dressing me up in party clothes, and allowing me to eat at the dining table, instead of alone, in pajamas, on a tray in my room, facing a wall.

Now that he was almost gone, I could remember, without wincing, his "jokes" about going to the movies to neck in the balcony. I could remember meeting Red and Uncle Charlie, Red laughing and hugging me, Red wanting to hear me talk about my mother. Whether my mother was in Europe, or if she had a gentleman caller, the same one as last month, or a different one. I could remember saying my mother was busy; not a business-woman, but a famous fashion designer. Telling Red how my mother dressed up in the morning to go to business. How she dressed up again at night. That was all I knew, of course. But Red never tired of hearing every little thing—what my mother wore, who the company was, when she had company. How I had always loved to tell; loved Red asking me so many questions. No one else ever asked me anything, not even my father. Not even now.

I remembered the time I came home early from the movies and found my mother already home, sitting up in her gray satin bed. She called me, and I went in to say good-night. She wrinkled her nose up and said, You've been with your father, he was smoking cigars, I can smell it in your hair.

I was with Red too, and Uncle Charlie, I said.

My mother's face looked dark, and then very white. I don't want him taking you with her, she shouted. You're not to go with them, do you hear me?

I didn't mean it! I said, flinching, backing away, running into my own room. My mother rang for the nurse.

Wash her hair! she shouted. Wash that disgusting smell out of her hair!

After that, I didn't go into my mother's room after the movies. She never asked me again if I'd seen Red and Uncle Charlie. I told my father what she had said, and he said, well, better not mention it when we run into them. Don't want to upset your mother.

I remembered the times Red and Uncle Charlie and my father and I stopped for sodas—and now suddenly I recalled my father squeezing Red's knee under the table, while Charlie smoked a big cigar that my father gave him. I had always thought we were all having fun. I thought that was family fun. Me slurping my soda, and making everyone laugh. It was painful to think how desperately I had wanted to live with them instead. How I had said that to Red, so many times. How much she liked hearing it. How foolish I was to think it meant she loved me.

At my father's funeral service, Red, the original one, came over to hug me. I would love to see you, sometime, she whispered. My mother, holding court, sat on the other side of the room, claiming the funeral, the death, like a widow. They had been apart forty years; each had remarried once and divorced again. Still, it was true she had survived him; my brother and I were the living proofs of her claim — not to any tangible thing, only to be here, holding court, wearing an elegant veiled hat, a black suit. People were offering her their condolences. Amazing. I would love to see you, Red said again to me, urgently.

Yes, I said. All right. I had not recognized her at first. Shocked to see her grown hugely fat. Still Red, though. The hair dyed now, like all the other imitation Reds.

We met at a coffee shop, a week later. I wanted to ask her about loving my father. Whether she really had; when she had stopped. Why.

I said that he had told me once, long ago, that he had at last asked her to leave Uncle Charlie and marry him. That he told me when it happened, after all those years of movies and ice cream sodas, golf games with Uncle Charlie, and dinners at their house and breakfast at the club and trips to Florida on the train, all of us, he and they, and I and their son who was almost exactly my age, and who looked—everyone whispered—almost exactly like my father. I said all of this to her, in the coffee shop.

And I said that when at last my father had asked Red to leave Charlie, leave her marriage for him, or else let him go, I knew she had turned him down flat. She had chosen Charlie, fat, dull, bald Charlie, instead. Charlie was dead now; he had been the first to die. Red had not seen my father for years, he would not forgive her. The moment she turned him down, I knew, he had stopped playing golf with Charlie, and gone off to find himself a new Red, the first of all the other women who would become Reds, to please him. So many of them had come to the funeral. I was sure she, too, was pleased by that, the original Red. Even if he had never forgiven her.

You won't believe this, she said to me now, in the coffee shop. I loved Charlie, I came to love him; in the end I realized I had loved him all along.

And my father?

Do you know, she said, your father never gave me anything? Not a flower. Not in twenty years.

I shook my head, as if to signify how terrible; that is terrible.

I often thought of you, she said then. All these years.

Really, I said.

We should see each other again. I know Billy—my son—you remember Billy—would like to know you now.

Billy wrote to me, after this. Things he remembered about my father, who had been Uncle Ed to him.

Unless my father was also, really, his father too. I didn't respond to Billy. I couldn't see Red again. I wanted to, but I couldn't. How could I ask her now, finally, if Billy was my brother, my twin? How could I not ask her? Why hadn't he come to the funeral? Better the deepening silence.

What struck me hardest was the thing she revealed so casually. In twenty years of adulterous passion, never even a flower!

I thought again of how when I was very young, he always sent a nosegay to me on my birthday, with the card signed *Affectionately, Dad.* Always the tight round bouquet of sweetheart roses in a paper lace collar, trailing slender ribbons of pink and blue satin. *Affectionately, Dad.* I remembered that on my real birthday, my real birth night, my mother, whose own mother died giving birth to her, labored alone, in her terror. My father was with Red, who was awaiting the birth of Billy.

A month after my father's funeral, I slipped on his elegant old watch. I realized I had no memory of him ever wearing it. A gift to him from Jo; a wedding gift. It was a sleek Art Deco design, all clean angles and beveled edges, with his initials in blue enamel on the gleaming clasp. White gold glows like silver or platinum, only warmer. Somehow it evoked my earliest images of him; it, too, had a wonderfully handsome face. A watch Cary Grant would have worn, teaching me how to meld in gin rummy, and to win the word game in the evening paper (Can you find

forty-six words of at least five letters in AFFECTIONATELY?
Alone, atone, cleft, natty, action, fatal, finale . . .).

I had the band made smaller, so the watch would circle my wrist lightly, an effortless embrace. I like to think he would notice that I always wear it, and would say that it suits me. I like to imagine him nodding. Affectionately.

Jo died three and a half years later, in 1982. I held a memorial service for her with the help of Parsons School, her alma mater, and the Fashion Institute of Technology. I invited all the old friends I could think of, and all the fellow designers who had known her at the beginning. Foxy came and whispered to me, *"She* made *something* of her life." It sounded strangely like a reproach. Then another friend, who I knew had an angry, troubled daughter, expressed surprise at my tears. *"Now,* you cry," she said bitterly. "I always cried," I said. "It was Jo who couldn't. These tears are for both of us."

Could she have been a greater success, a better artist, a loving human being, if she had had a mother like Gypsy Rose Lee's? A mother like mine? Or any mother at all but one who died giving birth to her?

After the memorial service, I went back to Jo's dazzling, silent apartment, with its thick white carpet, pale gleaming floors, and geraniums peering brightly through the terrace windows. Dominating the huge white room, as it had the yellow living room of my childhood, was the lovely oil painting of Jo, in its elaborate gilded frame. The portraitist had done Elsie de Wolfe and the Duchess of Windsor. He captured Jo in the twenties as a nineteenth-century Parisienne, her pale face luminous as a Renoir model's, under a black silk parasol.

In the hallway hung a smaller portrait, the old sepia-toned photograph of Minna Barrows Copeland, in its austere dark oval frame. I stood before one, then the other, gazing at two pairs of solemn dark eyes, the sensuous curve of two beautiful mouths. Two faces, so alike; two lives so mystifyingly different. Perhaps some simple, elegant message lay here for me, their survivor. The vibrant young woman who died giving life; the terrified, bereft child who sought an artist's escape from a woman's fate, but who became a mother in spite of herself. I had been given a strange legacy: fierce ambition, a passion for beauty, a talent for triumph over incalculable loss. Jo and I were both motherless daughters. Only Minna, the unknown one, might have taught us the beauty and passion of a mother's love. I grieved for us all.

FITTING

WRITING OF JO, I FOUND MYSELF SKETCHING
A SOFT FRENCH-BLUE JERSEY COSTUME, KICK-
pleated, with a fitted top that had gold thread woven with
the same blue wool in a luxurious, improbable hounds-
tooth pattern. The top flashed subtly when you moved,
and was only fully revealed when you took off the jacket.
The surprise of that kind of flashing was the way it made
you feel: as if you had a delicious secret. Any minute you
could let it out; everyone would gasp with pleasure.

I remember, too, a ring of white mink that seemed to
be the collar of a black wool suit—until the jacket came
off, and the fur was still there circling your throat, form-
ing a spectacular top to a sexy black halter dress. It was a
bestseller; she did two variations of it in successive collections.

There is a photograph of me wearing that halter dress, without the jacket. It was one of the few things of hers that we both owned, and loved, but it really looked better on her. I was quite grown up before it occurred to me that all designers look better in their own creations than anyone else does. This includes, I suspect, men who design for women.

I recall my mother's obituary crediting her with originating the two-piece suit. It wasn't a suit, exactly. It was this riff on the idea of a suit: the costume whose top was meant to be shed so you could show that you didn't really need it, that you looked even more stunning without it. Like the cliché movie scene in which the brainy secretary/teacher/librarian takes off her glasses and is suddenly a knockout, and never puts them on again.

It seemed a playfulness entirely absent in my mother's personality. Yet surely it must have been there, as well as in the clothes. Perhaps it was only that she never took off the jacket in my presence.

Once in a while, usually in a taxi, she would break into a whistle; it was a strange birdcall sort of sound, high and tremulous, lyrical and achingly sweet. Yet you couldn't follow the complex melody. It seemed to flow, a river of peculiar sound, pouring mysteriously from that perfectly shaped, perfectly red mouth, half-hidden in her silver-fox scarf, behind her dotted veil, above the loop of scarlet satin at her throat.

The taxi driver would turn in bewilderment.

"Was that you? Whistling?"

She would smile with pure delight. She was so seldom purely delighted. Only taxi drivers who commented on her whistling, or her perfume, or her elegance, ever seemed to earn that smile.

Eventually I, too, learned to whistle. An ordinary sound, air pushing a recognizable tune. But I have never heard anyone produce the extraordinary sound she made. Somehow that seems fitting.

ACKNOWLEDGMENTS

I had thought I would never attempt to write of my mother; of her mysterious, splendid life in fashion; of my own sad childhood at the dark fringes of that shining world. This book began by chance, through a chance meeting with Holly Brubach, fashion editor of *The New York Times Magazine*. We were strangers at a friend's art opening; we talked about the lost early stars of American fashion, of whom my mother was one, and about the need to jog memories of those pioneers, their struggle and their triumph. Days later, I found myself promising to jog my own memory, for Holly Brubach to publish in *The New York Times*.

It was the start of a journey and an exorcism, a discovery of searing light in the shadowed heart of my mother's dazzling success story—and of how that light danced in the beautiful city that was my mother's New York. In my child's eye, it was a city that seemed to be entirely hers, by her own design.

My first step, and Holly's decision to publish twice as many words as she had room for, led me still farther than I meant to go. The rest of the way I traveled with another stranger: the brilliant young editor Rob McQuilkin of Anchor Books. Rob was surer than I that I could go where the book would lead, and that I must. I am deeply grateful to Holly and Rob, and to my tireless, loving agent Charlotte Sheedy, as well as to the Writers' Room, that blessed sanctuary for New York writers who need to find a true voice; a place to search, alone yet not abandoned, in the city that swirls and sings its wild ceaseless chorus into our silences.

Finally, I thank my late husband, Robert E. Gould, who in his terrible final illness summoned the strength to attend my first reading from this book. His tears of pride and pleasure reassured me, as they always had, that the perilous journey will forever be the one to take. His fierce sweet courage sustained us both as I completed *Mommy Dressing*, in the last months of his life.

Lois Gould
March 1998

PHOTOGRAPHS AND ILLUSTRATIONS

Endpaper sketches (1920s) by Jo Copeland *(courtesy of the Fashion Institute of Technology Library)*

Jo Copeland drawing *(courtesy of the Fashion Institute of Technology Library)*

Jo Copeland with dress mannequin, circa 1969 *(courtesy of the Fashion Institute of Technology Library)*

Jo Copeland in France, early 1920s *(from the author's collection)*

Camille Roger and Hélène Thibault hat illustrations *(courtesy of Vogue, March 1, 1926. Copyright © 1926, renewed 1954, 1982, by Condé Nast Publications, Inc.)*

Gentleman and manservant illustration *(courtesy of Vogue, April 1, 1955. Copyright © 1955, renewed 1983, by Condé Nast Publications, Inc.)*

Jo Copeland dress advertisement *(courtesy of the Fashion Institute of Technology Library)*

Photograph of Lois Gould as a girl *(from the author's collection)*

Vanity mirror photograph *(courtesy of Vogue, May 1, 1945. Copyright © 1945, renewed 1973, by Condé Nast Publications, Inc.)*

Jo Copeland sequined dress advertisement *(courtesy of the Fashion Institute of Technology Library)*

Jo Copeland with Estee Lauder and Kitty Sokol at the opera *(courtesy of the Fashion Institute of Technology Library)*

Jo Copeland and friends on the boardwalk, Deauville, late 1920s *(from the author's collection)*

Jo Copeland *(from the author's collection)*

Jo Copeland, wearing the Art Deco ruby and diamond bracelets, photographed in Mambacher's Paris atelier, late 1920s *(from the author's collection)*

A Carson Pirie Scott millinery salon advertisement *(courtesy of Vogue/Condé Nast)*

Nurse and maid uniform illustrations *(courtesy of Vogue, March 15, 1926. Copyright © 1926, renewed 1954, 1982, by Condé Nast Publications, Inc.)*

Hosiery advertisement *(courtesy of Vogue/Condé Nast)*

Jo Copeland suit advertisement *(courtesy of the Fashion Institute of Technology Library)*

Jo Copeland fringed dress advertisement *(courtesy of the Fashion Institute of Technology Library)*